COACHING PRINCIPLES FOR THE DEVELOPMENT OF CHAMPIONSHIP TEAMS

ON AND BEYOND THE PITCH

HERBERT L. HOFFMAN PH.D.
& PETER R. J. FEWING

COACHING PRINCIPLES FOR THE DEVELOPMENT OF CHAMPIONSHIP TEAMS

ON AND BEYOND THE PITCH

HERBERT L. HOFFMAN PH.D.
& PETER R. J. FEWING

Common Ground

First published in Champaign, Illinois in 2010
by Common Ground Publishing LLC
at Sport and Society
a series imprint of The University Press

Library of Congress Cataloging-in-Publication Data

Hoffman, Herbert L.
Coaching principles for the development of championship teams : on and beyond the pitch / by Herbert L. Hoffman and Peter R.J. Fewing.

    p. cm.

Includes bibliographical references and index.
ISBN 978-1-86335-812-5 (pbk : alk. paper) -- ISBN 978-1-86335-813-2 (pdf : alk. paper)
1. Coaching (Athletics) 2. Coach-athlete relationships. 3. Teamwork (Sports) I. Fewing, Peter R. J. II. Title.

GV711.H636 2010
792.02'2--dc22

2010033551

For Patty Fewing, Father William J. Sullivan (Seattle University's 20th President),
Joe Zavaglia (Founder of Seattle University's Men's Soccer Program), Vince Volpe,
Dr. Joe Shamseldin (Team Physician), Mark Escandon (Athletic Trainer),
Assistant Coaches: Jeff Koch, Bill Collelo, Mike Collelo,
Frank Bartenetti, Matt Potter, Tom Hardy,
And all of Pete's student-athletes; especially those of the
1997 & 2004 National Championship Teams

Table of Contents

List Of Figures

Acknowledgments

Thanks to George Czarnowski, Craig Gauntt, Alex Chursky, Hans Esterhuizen, and John Fishbaugher for fully embracing this project and encouraging their teammates to do the same. Without their leadership and support, this book would never have been written. Thanks also to Dr. James Antony, Director of the University of Washington's Center for Leadership in Athletics, who suggested in the very early stages of this project that our book should tell stories. Thanks to Daisy Alfaro for transcribing Pete's stories. Lastly, thanks to Dr. Ed Taylor and Dr. Jennifer Hoffman who encouraged us to write this book.

Forward

I grew up in Lompoc, California. I had the good fortune of playing high school basketball and eventually the great fortune to go on and play at Gonzaga University. While in high school, I grew in the light of one of the greatest coaches of all time, John Wooden, and his guiding axioms:

"Failure is not fatal, but failure to change might be."

"It isn't what you do, but how you do it."

"It's not so important who starts the game but who finishes it."

In college, I played for Dan Fitzgerald, who was, in his own right, a legendary charismatic coach and citizen of the community. As I look back on my experiences, I am grateful to have met many coaches and learned something substantial from all of them. In my current role as a faculty member in the College of Education at the University of Washington (UW) and as Vice Provost and Dean of Undergraduate Academic Affairs at the UW, I have come to an explicit conclusion—coaches are educators, too.

To wit, education is about the acquisition of knowledge, the formation of the whole person, and developing the capacity for citizenship, self-awareness and awareness of the needs of others towards more decent communities and a more decent society. The word education comes from the Latin e-*ducere* meaning "to lead out."

So long as coaches are tasked with working with young men and women in our communities, they are accountable to some fundamental questions. What lessons are you teaching? What are your "students" learning? How do you know they are learning what you desire? Do the lessons have meaning beyond a particular moment in time?

Pete Fewing and Herbie Hoffman go about the work of demonstrating the power of coaching as a form of education. Through theory and narrative, they illustrate the power of lessons well taught and the power of intentional learning.

In the same year, two of the greatest coaches I have ever encountered have died. In keeping with the power of education, their legacy will live for generations to come. The onus of understanding, and extending, the impact of their lives as educators, lies with coaches of today.

The evidence of good teaching often manifests itself long after the actual formal teaching, whether in a classroom, on a soccer field, in a gymnasium, or in a theatre, is done. What will your students say about you at age 30, 40, 50 or beyond? Will your lessons add value to their lives as citizens, as parents, and as partners? Are we a better community because of your leadership? Your teaching? Hoffman and Fewing remind us that the answer to these questions comes with time.

Ed Taylor, Ph.D.
Associate Professor, College of Education
Vice Provost and Dean, Undergraduate Academic Affairs
University of Washington

Preface

Team sports teach athletes many valuable life lessons they can take with them beyond the field of play. Some lessons of note include commitment, teamwork, perseverance, goal setting, and good old-fashioned hard work. These lessons can't help but to be instilled in athletes. It is as if these lessons are embedded within sports. They are intrinsic. In addition to attaining these core components, I was fortunate enough to walk away with many other valuable life skills thanks to the leadership of Pete Fewing. Pete always preached the importance of "doing the right thing" at all times. Not just on the field, but more importantly, off the field. Treat people with respect, say please and thank you, take your hat off when entering a building, hold the door for strangers, and make your community a better place by volunteering, are just a few of the life lessons pounded into us during our years at Seattle U. Not until I grew older, did I truly understand and appreciate the importance of making those character traits a fundamental part of who I am. As I grow older, I still practice these beliefs in my everyday life. I value them and truly believe they make me a better person. As a 4th grade teacher, I teach these principles to my students in hopes of creating well rounded young children.

George Czarnowski
1997 NAIA National Champion, Most Valuable Player, & Team Captain
4th Grade Teacher

lect team coaching directors, this book is intended to describe the type of coaches they should be hiring and empowering.

Through the accessible stories of Peter Fewing, two-time men's national collegiate soccer coach[1] of the year and players from his Seattle University (Seattle U. / SU) national championship teams, the reader ultimately learns the vital leadership development role coaches can and should play during their student-athletes' formative years. All coaches should be modeling exemplary leadership and mentoring for their players. It is estimated that only 0.12% of high school student-athletes will become professional athletes. **Instead, the vast majority of student-athletes will become our future leaders in other professions.** Because of the significant role it plays in our young people's leadership development, coaching is a moral endeavor.

The stories of Coach Fewing and his national championship players illustrate how and why exemplary leadership and high team performance go hand-in-hand. Their collective voice explains why coaches should be embracing the concepts of authentic and transformational leadership. Research within the contexts of business and the military indicates that authentic leadership outperforms other leadership styles by consistently producing high performing teams. Teams led by authentic leaders time after time outperform those led via the "carrot or the stick" approach. This is why our nation's and other nations' military services strive to develop authentic leaders within their ranks (Avolio, & Gardner, 2005, Bass, 1985, 1996, 1998a, 1998b, 2000, Bass & Avolio, 1990, 1994, 2000, Dvir, Eden, Avolio & Shamir, 2002, Dvir & Shamir, 2003, Hoffman, 2010).

Can authentic leadership be modeled by athletic coaches for the benefit of preparing their student-athletes beyond the field of play? Is this style possible in a highly competitive setting? These questions were the original intent of studying Coach Fewing and his soccer program at Seattle University. A powerful story emerges in critically examining how and why Coach Peter Fewing[2] and his assistant coaches were able to win two national titles despite many obstacles beginning with inheriting a program which had lost eight seasons in a row. In his eighteen years of service, Fewing was able to also help raise 1.5 million dollars for a new stadium, develop two national players of the year, achieve nearly a 100 percent graduation rate of his student-athletes including one Rhode Scholar[3], twice receive Seattle University's President's award for campus leadership and establish the foundation for NCAA Division I soccer. His Seattle University teams consistently won because his primary focus for his student-athletes was beyond their playing days. As a former professional soccer player whose

---

1. 1997 NAIA National Coach of the Year, 1997 National College Soccer Coaches Association's Coach of the Year, 2004 National College Soccer Coaches Association Coach of the Year.

2. Pete's assistant coaches included Jeff Koch, Billy & Mike Colello, Frank Bartenetti, Matt Potter & Tom Hardy.

3. Ryan Sawyer

career did not last as long as he would have liked, Pete understood first-hand the difficult odds facing his aspiring student-athletes. Instead, Coach Pete prepared them for life beyond soccer by teaching them about leadership through his example.

What emerges from interviews conducted in 2009 with Coach Fewing and his players is that authentic transformational leadership is possible in a highly competitive athletic setting. The guiding leadership principles that Coach Fewing used to achieve authentic transformational leadership are shared. How and why these guiding leadership principles enabled Coach Fewing and his players to achieve great results both on and off the field of play are explored.

However, before examining how and why student-athlete coaches should be embracing authentic leadership through the example of Coach Fewing, it is necessary to review a general spectrum of the leadership literature that is focused on the leader-follower(s) relationship. This will enable a mapping of various coaching styles that our student-athletes have and continue to encounter.

Mapping Coaching Styles

A common theme that emerges across a review of leadership literature focused on the leader – follower(s) relationship is the concept of respect and consideration of others. This concept has grown from being non-existent in the initial concepts of leadership such as Machiavelli's (1988) *The Prince*[4] to being a foundational idea of the more recent conceptualizations of leadership. Beginning with McGregor's (1966) Theory Y of *The Human Side of Enterprise,* where people are viewed as people and not things to be manipulated, this foundational concept has been prominently featured and expanded upon. It forms the foundation of Burns' (1978) concept of transformational leadership and Foster's (1986) call for leadership to be critical, transformative, educative, and ethical. Respect and consideration of others is also the focal point for Greenleaf's (1977) concept of servant leadership and Gardner's (1990) call for followers to be looked upon as constituents and not followers. It is also prominently featured in the concept of authentic leadership (Brown & Trevino, 2006 & Gardner et al, 2005) and Leadership Member Exchange Theory (LMX) (Graen & Uhl-Bien, 1995).

---

4. "The end justifies the means." Machiavelli's concept means that such behavior as murder is justified if it keeps one in power.

Transformational leadership also includes concern for others, ethical decision-making, integrity, and role modeling. With an emphasis on vision, values, and intellectual stimulation, transformational leadership differs from ethical leadership's more transactional concern for moral management and "other" awareness (Brown & Trevino, 2006, pp. 598 - 600).

Leader-member exchange theory (LMX) (Graen & Uhl-Bien, 1995) is relationship-based, and explicitly focuses on how one-on-one reciprocal social exchanges between leader and follower evolve, nurture, and sustain the dyadic relationship. Although transformational and other leadership approaches predominantly concentrate on leader behaviors towards subordinates, the foundation of LMX research has been studying reciprocal exchanges between the leader and follower(s) (Wang et al, 2005, p. 420). The followers can influence the leader/coach as much as the coach can influence the followers. In LMX, the power of leadership can flow in both directions. A coach who embraces this concept does not view the power of leadership as his or her own to wield. A coach who embraces LMX theory possesses the most respect and consideration of others (Figure 1).

Exemplary Guiding Leadership Principles

To explain how and why exemplary guiding leadership principles are essential for a coach, the following chapters are organized around the stories of Coach Fewing and his players. Together they illustrate how and why a coach should be mindful that his or her players' stories are really his or her own story. A coach who adheres to these authentic leadership principles in thought and action will consistently develop high performing teams.

Chapter One explores the thoughts of Coach Pete's players on why they won their respective national championships. Chapter Two illustrates that the development of a high performing team all starts with the coach realizing that he or she is ultimately responsible for all that happens with the team. She or he is the one who must be the one who sets, maintains, and ignites the team's vision. Chapter Three explains why a coach should strive to cultivate an environment where everyone is a leader and everyone matters. A coach who embraces this concept not only recognizes the power of informal leadership but continuously looks for opportunities for it to flourish. A coach who preaches and practices this belief in his or her interactions with their team understands this principle is the critical element to foster high esprit de corps within the team. High esprit de corps is a foundational characteristic of a high performing team. Why every detail matters is the focus of Chapter Four. A coach who ensures that all the little details are paid attention to and consistently analyzed will have more success than those that don't have such discipline. The development of a high performing team hinges on the coach being mindful of the details and also their own bias when analyzing the details. Chapter Five illustrates that as much as a coach needs to believe in the principle of everyone is a leader and everyone matters, she or he must also understand there are non-negotiable behavioral expectations of being a team member. If a team member or team mem-

bers consistently violate team community, a leader must address their behavior. Otherwise, their behavior will tear apart the team and become the
norm. Chapter Six discusses why a coach needs to understand that highly
successful student-athletes have a focused passion for what they do. Focus
and passion are not mutually exclusive. A coach must monitor the team's
behavior particularly when things are going well. Chapter Seven illustrates
why a coach must fundamentally understand what his or her team's mission
is and what success looks like. It is essential that a coach views all of her or
his team's activities through this lens to evaluate if they are value added or
not. A leader who keeps his or her team centered on what is important understands that a highly effective leader shields his or her team from unnecessary activities that can inhibit the team to reach its full potential. Chapter
Eight exemplifies that language and stories are some of the most powerful
tools a coach has available to them as they strive to develop their team into a high performing one. Using leadership and student development literature, Chapter Nine explains how and why Coach Fewing's leadership style
was highly successful in developing high performing teams of student-athletes on and beyond the pitch.

Chapter 1

Deep Commitment to Each Other was the Tipping Point

Introduction

To understand what the key elements were that produced national championship teams, the players of both the 1997 and 2004 teams[5] were separately asked a simple open-ended question: "Why did we win?" Whether they were team captains, national players of the year or role players, the players' responses from and across both teams remained consistent.

---

5. Both teams have been inducted into Seattle University's Athletic Hall of Fame.

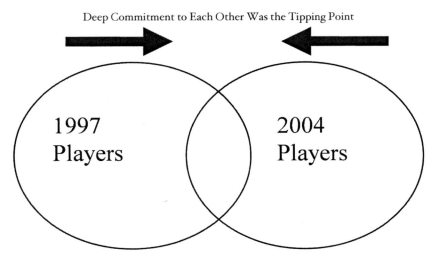

Figure 2: "Why did we win stories?"

The theme that emerged across all of the players' responses was that they won because they committed to each other as a team. They became a family who held each other to a high standard both on and off the field. "It was about doing things right both on and off the soccer field" and "it was about taking the game of soccer seriously which made soccer so much fun to play" (Stan Thesenvitz, 1997 National Champion). Continuously encouraging and challenging each other to improve, nothing else mattered except playing and desiring to win for each other.

George Czarnowski, a team captain who scored the game winning goal in the overtime of the 1997 national championship final, shares his thoughts on why his teammates were able to win.

> We won because we believed in each other. Each guy on the team had a role to play. Each guy's role was no more important than anyone else's role. Every role was different, but every role was equally important to the overall success of the team, because if one guy didn't do his part, then the rest of the team couldn't do theirs. I knew I could count on my teammates to do their jobs and they count on me to do mine. I knew that if I passed the ball out to the wing to Arne or An, I knew they would try everything in their power to get down the line and send a cross in. If the other team crossed the ball into our penalty box, I knew one of our defenders would do everything in their power to get to the ball first and clear it out. We didn't want to let each other down and a great example of that can be illustrated in this story.

> After the national final when 5 to 6 of us were sitting around reflecting on the game, someone brought up the question of what you were thinking during the overtime period. I recall answering the question the following way. 'I was thinking that there was no way I was going to let the guy I was guarding, score a goal. I didn't want to be the guy who let up for one second and let my team-mates down. I would have run through a brick wall to ensure I didn't let my teammates down.' As I was giving the answer I saw every other guy sitting there nodding his head up and down. Some guys laughed and said they were thinking the exact same thing (George Czarnowski, 1997 National Champion & Team Captain).

Santa Maria Rivera, a team captain of the undefeated 2004 national championship team echoes George's thoughts. Santa shares that the reason his team won was because of an unwavering will to play and win for each other.

> We won because we were hungry, and not for W's or championships, but for greatness. We were ambitious, we not only wanted to win every time we stepped on the soccer pitch, but we wanted to dominate every game and every aspect of the game. We wanted to leave no doubt in our opponents mind once they stepped off the pitch that they got outworked, outhustled, and outclassed. We excelled at the little things that year. We had the killer instinct to put teams away, and whenever we got ourselves into a hole we would always dig together. We won because after not allowing a goal for 7 straight games, we wanted it to be eight. We won because of our unwavering will to win and play for each other (Santa Maria Rivera, 2004 National Champion & Team Captain).

Tom Hardy, 1997 National Player of the Year, shares that his team deeply cared about each other. Tom states that this was the key difference from his previous years' teams which had an equal level of talent. Everyone on the 1997 team fully embraced and understood their team role.

> The 1997 SU team won the national title for a number of reasons. There were growing pains, however, along the way to the championship season. The case can be made that the 1995 and '96 teams were just as talented of a group of players, but for one reason or another didn't put everything together throughout an entire season. The '97 team all cared about each other, both on and off the field, and enjoyed being around one another. This was a bit of a change from years past when things weren't always harmonious. Everyone knew their role on the '97 team, from the seniors to the freshman, and starters to the reserves. The junior and senior classes were made up of experienced players who took leadership roles, focusing the team when things got off track (Tom Hardy, 1997 National Champion & National Player of the Year).

Like Tom Hardy, Bobby McAlister, 2004 national player of the year, shares that his team's commitment to each other was much deeper than in previous years. In Bobby's mind, this was the key ingredient in enabling his team to reach its full potential. Similar to the 1997 team, Bobby thought that this was the key difference from teams he had been on in previous years which had equal levels of talent. No matter what their role was, everyone on the 2004 team equally embraced the same goal. Bobby attributes this to Coach Pete's leadership.

> Looking back, one of the main differences in the team was not the talent level. The talent level in previous years was as high as 2004, but there was a buy-in that we had never had before. Those that played every minute and those who played few all had the same vision and same dream. This is rare to find at any level of competition, let alone at a high collegiate level. This was in part from Coach Pete. Every player believed in Pete and he in turn believed in us. This trust took us a long ways, and in my mind set the groundwork for us to achieve what we never would have dreamed (Bobby McAlister, 2004 National Champion & National Player of the Year).

Commitment to the team concept was the tipping point for Craig Gauntt. A key role player in 1997, Gauntt shares that his team won because of a deep commitment and belief in each other.

We 'won' because of a commitment to the team concept. This commitment to the team and our teammates, cultivated a team chemistry that was incredibly strong. This commitment ultimately produced a belief in ourselves and as a collective group - that regardless of the opponent, score or situation – we simply knew we'd win the game. This belief in winning with the foundation of talent, commitment and chemistry was fundamental in our success.

Commitment to the team centered on the idea about holding yourself and your teammates to a higher standard of achievement. The notion of holding ourselves and each other to a 'higher standard' could be seen on and off the field. Guys pushed each other on the field, yet we also held each other to a higher standard in regards to conduct, academics and athletic achievement. The program was not about 'settling' or moral victories (Craig Gauntt, 1997 National Champion).

Jason Bressler shares similar thoughts as Craig Gauntt. A key role player in 2004, Bressler believes the deep-rooted bond his teammates had as friends enabled them to win.

Like all champions, success is a manifestation of hard work, dedication, skill, and little bit of luck. While each of these factors played a vital role in our success, none completely set us apart from the rest of the country. What did, however, was our desire to play for one another not only as teammates, but as friends...When our captain broke his leg, it wasn't just our duty to him as players to win, but our duty as friends as well. Although our offense was deadly and our defense nearly impenetrable, it was our bond as friends that made us national champions (Jason Bressler, 2004 National Champion).

Jake Besagno, a four year starting defender, shares that the 2004 team played and desired to win for each other. He shares that the team's esprit de corps was extremely high both on and off the field during the 2004 season. As a result of this, the sole motivation of everyone was to play for each other no matter what their role. Jake shares that this deep commitment to each other enabled all of his teammates to maintain a disciplined focus which he believes is vital to win a national championship.

My personal opinion on the reason that we won in 2004 and the reason that we went undefeated during that season was because the team played for each other rather than worrying about how many wins, how much playing time we got, what awards we were going to receive etc. I can honestly say that I can't remember once during the season when I said to myself so and so shouldn't be playing or 'we absolutely need to win this game' and turned my attention towards that rather that focusing on playing my best. We as a team were confident in our ability as a team and knew that as long as we worried only about our own game, we would win no matter how long we had to play. On the field we were a classy team, one that didn't resort to cheap shots, or dirty play, rather we were a team of players that relied on our ability and work rate to secure wins. We were never a flashy team or one that played with fancy flicks and footwork but a team of simplicity, hard work, and camaraderie.

Off the field we were an extremely close knit team. We took classes together, ate together in the lunch room and typically hung out together whenever possible...As far as staying focused off the field, the 2004 season was one that all players remained disciplined. There were no big parties even after big wins over University of Portland, University of Washington, Seattle Pacific University, and our win that sent us to the final four. We would often get together after games and hang out but rarely drank or did anything that would hamper us from playing our best at the next training session (Jake Besagno, 2004 National Champion).

Tate Miller, a starting defender on the 1997 team echoes Besagno's thoughts on why they won.

> We won because we were a team. We lived together, spent social time together, most of us played for four years together in the same system with the same coach. Most importantly we had fun doing it...We were a family and still are a family (Tate Miller, 1997 National Champion).

Arne Klubberud, a starting outside midfielder and teammate of Miller's shares that the tipping point of their 1997 national championship season run was their deep commitment to each other. This was brought about by the realization that they had only one season left together.

> I think the reality is a lot of things came together perfectly - chemistry, leadership, desire, talent, and luck. For three years, we had underachieved. The night after we lost our final game to Simon Fraser and the 3rd time in a row in the regional final, the frustration was clear. The past two years, there was joy when the season ended. That year, it was a realization that we had one season left and we had wasted an opportunity. We made the commitment that night to be successful on and off the field (Arne Klubberud, 1997 National Champion).

The theme of deep commitment to each other as the tipping point continues. Jason Cascio, a freshman starting defender on the 2004 team, shares his thoughts on the key reasons behind winning the national championship. Team commitment is demonstrated through hard work and playing for each other not only as teammates but as family members. For Cascio, team and family are one in the same.

> The reason we won is because we were a true example of what it means to be a team. All the way from Pete our head coach to a red shirt freshman – we were a cohesive group. From day one that I walked into the program our team took pride in being a family. Pete was like the father, the other coaches were just another head of the household and all of us players were their children. As a side note I thought one of the reasons we were so successful as a team was because all of the coaches brought something unique to the table. Pete was the head honcho that everyone looked up to and respected and wanted to work and win for while Potter and Bill were the guys you could go to and joke around and have a few laughs. As far as the team goes, as a freshman I looked up to all the upper classman and I didn't truly know what the college life and college game was about. Therefore there was one thing that stuck out in my mind is the fact that I just wanted to win and do well for the upper classman. We won because we were a team of great individual players who put themselves aside and played for the person next to them. Another reason why we won is because we worked our asses off on the practice field so the games seemed easier then our practice (Jason Cascio, 2004 National Champion).

Pat Doran, a four year starter during his playing days, echoes the theme of deep team commitment as why they won. Doran cites that team commitment enforced by the coach and the players themselves as the reason why his team won a national championship and went undefeated in 2004.

The single most significant factor for the team's success was our unwavering commitment, not only towards achieving our goals, but to our teammates and coaches. Coach Fewing established a set of commandments to help us focus on maximizing our potential and avoid any actions that would be detrimental to the team. Coach Fewing would often quiz us before, during or after practice to make sure we knew each guideline word for word. He would say something to the effect of, 'Hey Doran, what's rule #3?' I remember getting extremely annoyed with repeatedly hearing these guidelines, but now I understand their importance (e.g. 'Be a gentleman', 'Don't do anything to harm yourself or your team', etc). We had team captains and experienced leaders that did not tolerate negative behavior and held each other accountable for our actions (Pat Doran, 2004 National Champion).

Conclusion

Both teams shared that talent is not enough. It helps a great deal but is not enough to consistently win; particularly when the level of competition is extremely challenging. Both teams learned this lesson in the years prior to their national championship runs.

...Both the 1996 and the 2003 teams would be the first to admit that they underachieved. They underachieved because of a lack of complete commitment to each other and to the success of the team. It was okay and good to rally and beat the Huskies (University of Washington). But it didn't matter if we didn't beat lesser teams because we'd had already proven ourselves. There was a lack of commitment to doing it right every single time and a lack of commitment to each other and also a lack of commitment to their own behavior (Peter Fewing).

Talent Alone Doesn't Lead to Success

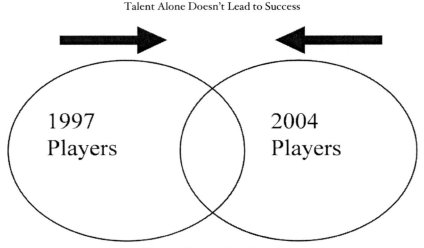

Figure 3: Talent is Not Enough

As shared by the players of both national championship teams, a deep commitment to the concept of team is the tipping point. Along with talent, it creates an athletic program that wins championships.

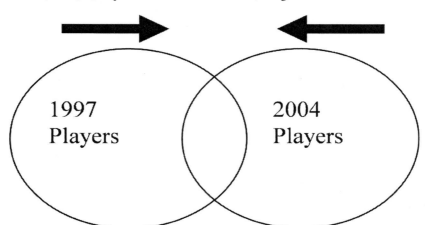

(Talent) + (Deep Commitment to Each Other) = High Team Performance

Figure 4: The Equation for High Team Performance

At levels of intense competition, this knowledge is pivotal as coaches strive to get the best out of their players. As such, a main purpose of this book is to share Peter Fewing's insights how he and his assistant coaches were able to consistently cultivate an environment where deep team commitment is fostered. Fostering deep team commitment is the leadership challenge of coaching. Although extremely difficult to achieve, it starts with the head coach. As shared by the players of Seattle University's (SU) men's national championship soccer teams of 1997 and 2004, deep team commitment not only fuels but strengthens a team's collective will to win, its resiliency. Deep team commitment was repeatedly cited as the main reason why they won their respective national championships. In years prior, both teams had the relatively same talent level as their national championship teams but did not reach their dream of winning a national championship until they fully grasped, internalized, and consistently demonstrated in their actions an unwavering commitment to each other.

Chapter 2
It's Up to You

Introduction

In this chapter, Coach Pete describes how it was up to him to develop Seattle University's men's soccer program into a highly successful one, despite having eight bosses in nine years and an ever changing athletic affiliation (NAIA to NCAA Division III to NCAA Division II). Although surrounded by poor and unengaged leadership that embraced mediocrity, Pete did not waver in his quest to win a national championship or use it as an excuse. Pete ultimately knew that the catalyst of success for the men's soccer program was him. This drove him in everything he did from scheduling challenging Division I opponents to building team benches and a respectable scoreboard. The guiding principle of "It's Up to You" enabled Pete to cultivate a team environment necessary to win two national championships during this time span. It also enabled him to raise funds for a new field and get his team to be sponsored by Nike.

Eight Bosses in Nine Years

You had eight bosses in your last nine years during the team's most successful seasons. How did you deal with constantly changing leadership? How were you able to create a winning culture in the absence of leadership? Can you talk a little bit how you were able to do so? Please describe.

The first ten years we had one A.D. (athletic director) and then after that we had a series of bosses that came and went. They were interim bosses or bosses that we had for six months. At the ten year point was actually when we won our first national championship. So the bosses we had never set standards for expectations of wins, losses, and fundraising. You had to be on budget, but there was no vision set forward by them that made us say, "Ok, we've got to do this, we've got to do that." So as the bosses came and went on such a quick turnaround, there was no vision. The bosses were there really just to make sure that we were on task: budget-wise and that we followed the rules. After that, it was "Good luck." But the good news was you were allowed to build your program as you felt it should be.

There was never true leadership, in those eight bosses in nine years - and it was not a problem - I never saw it as a detriment because I didn't know any different. I never had leadership that said, "How can we help?" I just knew it was up to me to create a winning culture.

For example, I'll never forget, we had beaten the Washington Huskies in my third year of coaching there. The year before I got there, in 1987, the Huskies beat Seattle U., 8 to 0. And then our first year that we were there, in '88, we lost 4 to 0. And the second year we lost 2 to 1 and then we won 1 to 0 in my third year. It was a big deal. And I'll never forget it. This sums up the whole problem; my boss walked by the office door three times and on the third time I just said, "Hey!" And the A.D. said, "Yeah?" I said, "We beat the Huskies yesterday!" The A.D. just gave me a thumbs up and said, "Good job." It was sort of just one of those things where you shake your head and go, "Ok" [sighs]. Getting the game against the University of Washington for Seattle University at that time was a bit of a win, so winning the game actually was huge. The A.D. had no idea we won, let alone played them.

You were able to win two national titles during this time span. Can you talk about the first time you really decided that you were going to win a national championship?

I distinctly remember talking about winning a national championship in my first week on the job. I remember talking about winning a national championship in staff meetings and people afterwards saying, "You've got to be nuts that you would even be talking about that." But because cross-town rival Seattle Pacific University had won five national championships, it did not seem unattainable. Also, Simon Frasier had won national championships up in Canada and we played them each year. So, it didn't seem out of the grasp. It didn't seem like it was impossible to do. It seemed very possible. And after we won it, and after reflecting on it now I look at it and I think- especially that first one...How the heck did we pull that off?

Prior to my first year, the soccer program had had eight losing seasons in a row. My first year was its ninth losing season in a row. That year I brought Jason Weighter from Duke University out to meet the players. He had just won the championship in '86. I had Jason show all the guys his championship ring so they could envision winning.

What role did your bosses play, for example, in getting the Nike sponsorship?

Beyond signing the final agreement, not too much. We just hustled on that one as we did in everything. The Nike contract is something I'm very proud of because we earned our value to Nike over a long period of time. We worked very hard. We used my soccer camp[6] as sort of leverage to make the Nike deal better. My camp bought a lot of product, i.e. soccer balls, t-shirts, staff gear, etc., and so, in return Nike gave us a lot of product, i.e. uniforms, shoes, staff gear, etc. to Seattle U. All NCAA legal but the only part of the equation on the Nike deal was that the boss signed the contract after it was all negotiated. I went to Oregon a lot to meet with Nike. The only time that the A.D. got involved was near the end of my time at Seattle University, when they tried to cut the contract. My last A.D. tried to take away our contract. They tried to get rid of my portion which was some merchandise, but after years with a relationship with Nike, Nike stood behind me and insisted that not be changed. That was the only time that they were a part of the negotiation. They let us run our program as long as we weren't breaking any rules, and you know, we just decided it was up to us. We were entrepreneurs I guess.

The fire that burned to win national championships - where did that come from?

That came from the inside. That was from us; the players and the coaches. The coaches set the mission and the vision, and the players rose to the occasion. It took us a long time to get there. You know it took a long time for Mike Krzyzewski at Duke. It took a long time for John Wooden at UCLA. It took us ten years like I think it took Wooden sixteen. But there wasn't, "How do we do this? How do we help you with attendance? How do we help you with scheduling" Fundraising was left up to you to raise money for any extras you wanted for the program. We sold t-shirts, we sold stadium bricks. I went out and got sponsorship money. I remember one day saying, we need to have ten thousand bucks by June 30th and we got it.

How about your ideas of renovating the field - can you talk a little bit about that?

Yes, when we got the new field started in 1996 it was first called the East Field. It was a great grass field with very simple bleachers. It was junior highish though with its three fifty aluminum seat sections that were not elevated. They just sat in the middle of the field on the sideline and it just didn't look very collegial. It didn't look very inviting. The field itself was great but the surroundings were very below the standard of Seattle University. We wanted our program to be of a high standard. We started trying to work on it about 2000. Then Vince Volpe came in and he was one of the first to notice the field was sub-par and there were some safety issues. We had two

6.http://www.peterfewingssoccercamp.com/

baseball backstops right next to the field. The backstops were there because the community wanted us to have backstops. It was part of the conditions in getting the field approved but they were never used. So we just started to say, "Let's re-build this into something special." And then over time it went forward.

But, originally, I remember this idea wasn't really well received. Correct?

Correct.

Can you describe that?

Yes. We slowly, but surely started to say, "Let's change this, let's make it something special. Let's make it a place that reflects our Seattle U. soccer program." At first, I remember sitting in meetings and every time I'd come up with an idea, it was shot down, and if I said we should do one thing it never got anywhere. I was the one who actually came up with the idea to renovate the stadium but at every turn, I was dismissed. Jeff Gervin who was the architect - a great guy who unfortunately has passed away, called me one day. Actually, I called him and said, "Can we get together?" I wanted to find out what it would take to build it and how much it would cost. It was just the two of us. I was going to buy him lunch because I couldn't pay him for any information, a quote or anything. I didn't have the authority to hire him, but we hit it off. We became good friends. We hung out a little bit together. He came to our property in North Bend and to our house in Seattle. We developed a nice rapport. He started saying, "You give me your ideas and I'll present them." So once Jeff started presenting our ideas, they started gaining traction. Again, I had no idea what to do since this was the first time I'd ever developed anything. But it seemed logical to get plans drawn up that we could show people. I remember paying about 175 dollars out of my own pocket to buy and laminate pictures of a rendition of what the new stadium would be. I made about six or seven copies. I gave one to the athletic director. I gave one to the women's soccer coach. And I went out and started trying to make it happen. It was like I was pushing a rock up the hill. I remember at one point, a prominent administrator saying, "This will never happen." And six years later it did happen [laughs].

There's more than one way to skin a cat, you know. Vince Volpe came along and was a terrific leader. Joining Vince was Joe Zavaglia, a banker, mentor, and friend who as a freshman started Seattle University's soccer program in 1967. Between Joe and Vince, we had a team the university believed in. They could do a lot of other things for the school. Eventually because of my relationship with Vince and Joe, we all came together with a vision. We brought in some other people to the vision. Because of who Vince was, the university wanted to make Vince happy, plus Vince was going to support it. Before Vince, it took six years to get to the point where it was priority number thirteen. And then like bamboo, it took a week to go from thirteen to number one.

There's a similar path between going from what we had field wise, to our national championships. At my house, I actually made benches out of wood for the team. I also made a scoreboard out of wood for the team. These were for the old intramural field which was in a different location to where the field is today. I don't know of any other college soccer stadium today, where there is covered seating. The paths of going from an intramural field to what Championship Field is today, to have the field renamed and called Championship Field for the two men's soccer national championships, and going from eight losing season's in a row to a national championship mentality were all similar processes. The vision was there. We never gave up on the vision. We just kept pushing. And it was a good thing. It was a good thing! Also, it wasn't like we were looking to get cars, do anything outside the boundaries of what is ethical, what is moral and all that. We wanted the guys to be great student-athletes. We wanted to provide a meaningful experience for them. We wanted them to win a national championship and have a great place to play.

Can you again talk a little bit about the leadership you had above you. You were also going Division III from the NAIA and then the University decided to go Division II. So can you put all of your efforts into building a high quality program given this context?

Yes, so when we were in the NAIA we had 2.4 scholarships I believe. And it slowly but surely got a little bit better. But then there was a movement to go Division III, where there are no scholarships. I'll never forget the meeting we had with the players in January of '96. We had the meeting in the Astro-gym - an indoor training facility on campus, with all the guys. I said, "Well we're going into Division III." It was a real sad day. Because you know, we're still going to be a soccer team. We're still going to play in a league. But we were going with no scholarships. And it meant then that we were probably going to join a league that would curtail some of our other games that we enjoyed like the University of Washington, the University of Portland, etc.

So that was the university's vision to align with small private Northwest schools?

Yes, it was the vision to align SU with the small independent colleges which is fair enough. But most Jesuit schools are Division I. So that's where we wanted to go. Division I or Division III which people said was the best fit. I remember Craig Gauntt specifically asking about how going to Division III was going to impact our team... I just told Craig and the team, "Hey, let's just win a national championship. This isn't going to affect your time at Seattle U. So let's just win a national championship and see where it lands." And they all kind of said, "Ok." That was explaining to them we got bad news, we're going to Division III and you know, yada, yada, yada. But this won't affect you guys. So let's win a national championship and see what they do. That was in January '96 after the Board of Trustees vote.

So, we started losing scholarship money. This meant that for the '96 season we didn't have scholarships for our incoming freshman class. In the '97 season, we didn't have money for our freshmen and sophomores. We only had two scholarships that were divided amongst the juniors and seniors on the team. That was the year we won the first national championship. The next year we went to the final four and lost in the semis. For those very close to the team, they thought this season was even better than our '97 run since with that group; we only had scholarships for the seniors. That was quite a big deal.

I distinctly remember when the decision was made and SU went Division III, someone high up in the administration saying, "Well this will be good. We'll get better student-athletes." But the reality was that the guys we had on scholarships were already good student-athletes. The list of our guys going to reputable graduate schools like Georgetown, Notre Dame, NYU, USC, and Virginia is long. We were not dumb jocks. It wasn't just about athletics. And then the success on the field...the combination of how they did academically and the success on the field I think, helped bring the university back to a place where they said let's go NCAA Division II.

How about the wins against the Division I (DI) programs? How did they contribute to the university deciding to go Division I at the end of the day?

Yes, I would say that we would give the players credit for this. We tried hard to schedule as many DI programs as we could. I called Notre Dame at one point. Stanford also...

But it was really you. Not the athletic directors or any- Right?

Oh yes. Nobody said, "You got to go schedule these guys." As a matter of fact, it was never questioned why we were scheduling those guys. Basketball wasn't allowed to schedule Division I programs at one point because they didn't want to look bad and get beaten. But for men's soccer, there was never a restraint. We were already beating Division I programs.

Who were they?

We beat University of San Francisco. It was great. They were number five in the country when we beat them. We beat them 2-1 in overtime. And we beat the University of Washington a couple of times. And then, Gonzaga [chuckles]. We beat Gonzaga repeatedly to the point that they didn't want to play us anymore. I don't remember losing very much to Gonzaga in the last ten years I coached. The University of Portland always beat us but we beat them the last time we played them. We finally did crack that nut [chuckles]. And for me, playing the best programs, playing against the best talent was just the best way to improve the team. The guys learned what it would take to win against stiff competition. No one ever took it easy on us. We had some pretty intense battles. With Portland, it was fun because one year we lost 3-2 in overtime. They scored the third goal with minutes to go. And then sometimes, it'd be five-nothing and they just absolutely crushed us [laughs]. You know, they were such a good team and if you weren't real good, real sharp when you came in, it was going to be a long day.

But no one was saying, "Go play these teams." No one was saying, "Go get this Nike contract." No one was saying, "Go after the top talent." No one was saying, "You know, let's build this facility." No one was saying, "How do we make this thing special?" That was never encouraged. No one was ever saying, "Why don't you get involved in the community? Why don't you go have the players show up at the University's Fundraising Gala and do something?" Whenever we had a building dedication on campus, I'd make the team go. And no one was saying, "You got to do that." It's just that we had a vision for where the program was going to be and where the stance of the program should be. And the players bought in. **They bought in because they knew that we were working as hard as they were. And even a little bit harder. They bought in because they knew that we cared about them.**

Bobby McAlister who was the National Player of the Year in 2004 shares similar thoughts regarding the importance of deep team commitment being the driving force behind their team's success. For Bobby, deep team commitment starts with the coach.

...We won the National Championship and did it the right way. We worked hard, believed in each other, and earned every accolade our team received. Lessons learned from this experience will be taken with us for the rest of our lives. Every player on that team will no doubt be successful in their lives after soccer. Seeing how hard you have to work to achieve a team goal is something that many people will never understand. It is hard to even think back to the 2004 season because it makes you miss the camaraderie you have with your teammates. It truly is something you cannot replicate in any other situation. But, to achieve the highest level and never lose a single game is truly something special. There is also something to be said about achieving a goal without being able to truly see it. It is no fluke that Pete was at the helm of two National Championship teams. Aside from everything else I have talked about, every player on our team believed in Pete and wanted to play hard for him. Every player gave everything they had to play for Pete. This is a very rare thing to have a coach who every player believes completely in. I know every player from that team has a bond that will never be broken and have had memories which no one can take away from us (Bobby McAlister, 2004 National Player of the Year).

Summary

Coaching is a moral endeavor for it involves and shapes student-athletes' lives. Therefore, a coach is charged to create the best environment for team success. No matter the surrounding environment, this is the case. Instead of waiting and depending on others, it truly is up to you. This is evident in Pete's stories of striving to develop a winning culture despite constant indifference and turnover of his bosses. Transformation into a high performing team starts first and foremost with the coach. As Bobby McAlister shares, the coach must be the catalyst.

Chapter 3
Everyone is a Leader, Everyone Matters[7]

Introduction

Through the stories of Stevie Jenkins, Hans Esterhuizen, Nick McClusky, and Jordan Inouye, Pete illustrates how a coach's embracement of the principle, "Everyone is a Leader, Everyone Matters" enables a team to develop into a high performing one. A coach who embraces this guiding principle understands that it is his or her job to cultivate an environment where esprit de corps can thrive. Esprit de corps fuels the team to reach its full potential. As shared by both the 1997 and 2004 players, it was the team's full embracement of this principle (from starters to role players to players that saw little to no time game time) that enabled high success.

Can you talk about a couple of players that you feel illustrate "Everyone is a Leader, Everyone Matters?"

---

7. "Everyone is a leader, Everyone Matters" is the same guiding leadership principle that elite military units like the Rangers expect out of all of their soldiers. Everyone from top to bottom is viewed as a leader.

Stevie Jenkins

Yes. First off what comes to mind having been away now from coaching for a little bit, I can tell you that that when I go back to coaching I will definitely recognize this point even more so. Some of the leaders on our team that didn't score goals or save goals or set up goals had an equally important value to the team. There were guys like Steve Jenkins who right now as we speak is in the hospital. Today is January 3, 2009. On December 31, 2008, we sat in his hospital room and he was saying, "I'm not going to take it any more care." He was ready to die. And thank God, he's come back a little bit. He's a young man with Cystic Fibrosis (CF) who came to our program. I played soccer for his dad.

In 1987, we were on a tour in England and his dad said to me, "No God. There's no God. No God would let little kids die of diseases." Stevie had been diagnosed with CF at age three, which is a terrible disease and as he got older it got worse. By the time Stevie was a senior in high school; his health had started to decline quite a bit. We knew that Stevie's health wasn't great. We recruited him because a buddy of mine suggested it while we were on the sidelines.

The process with Stevie was that we recruited him knowing that he probably wouldn't play a role on the field. But we recruited him because like Ian Walsh, we could give a kid an opportunity. We also knew that there's an existential leadership component that you get from a player like Steve Jenkins where he teaches people about the good of life. The value of life. The importance of life. The fragility of life. Just by his presence of his life. So the way it happened was I saw him play when he was eighteen. I had contact with parents: Tom and BJ Jenkins on and off throughout his childhood. Like I said, I played for his dad in the late eighties for FC Seattle. When I saw Stevie play in 2003, I went over to his mom, BJ and said hello. We talked for a little bit and I asked how he was doing. She gave me an update. Stevie wasn't doing great but he was still on the team and he could warm up. So, I went back to a buddy of mine, Brian Klein and told him the story of how difficult Stevie's journey has been. I shared with Brian that Stevie's prognosis had been that he wouldn't make it to the age of eighteen and now he is eighteen. Brian said, "You got to make a spot for him on your team at Seattle U." I thought that's a great idea. We're a Jesuit School. You know, why not? Why not!?! So we did. I called BJ the next day and said, "You know, BJ, what do you think? Do you think Stevie would be interested in playing at Seattle University? You know, go to school there?" And the thing that I was always so impressed was Stevie had something like a 1280 SAT score and a 3.85 GPA. I know it was at least above a 3.85; somewhere in that area. I would not have been a serious student or a good student if I knew my health was like his but Stevie was very committed and dedicated. He had a vision and a plan that he was going to live a long time. The eighteen-year window he'd been given was not his view. BJ said "Well, yeah. We, you know, Seattle would be great, but we can't afford it. We've got to save all our money because he's going to have to have a lung transplant at Stanford. We're going to have to be down there for six months. We've got to save every penny we can." And I said, "Well we're a Jesuit school. Surely our president will give him a full ride." And then I went and met with the president and we got him a full ride. So, I went back to Stevie and I said, "Hey"- and then we started the recruiting process.

When I met with Fr. Steve Sundborg, Seattle University's president, we had about a thirty-minute window to meet. He's a busy man. The first twenty-five minutes were about something else, I don't recall. And then he looked at his watch and said, "I got to get going." And I said, "Well there's one other thing." I literally had four minutes I think, to talk to him. I just started explaining Stevie's story and I got very choked up about this young man. Fr. Sundborg was not comfortable with me being choked up in his office. And so, he said, "What do you want?" I said, "He needs a full ride." So he said, "Ok, ok we'll get that."

It was just a flat out full ride. So, I'll always be grateful to Fr. Sundborg for that because that was a big deal. So, we went back to Stevie's parents to tell them we got a full ride. I think in the back of my mind, I knew that this would pay off in many, many ways. It would teach the players so much. It would be good for the program. Stevie's story was in the front page of *The Seattle Times* not too long ago. I knew that it would come out eventually.

I just knew that it would be a win-win. I also knew it was the Jesuit Mission statement in action. It was the coming to fruition of that mission statement. You know, helping somebody out. One of the things that I kind of wanted- I did not want my own name tied to it, too much to be quite honest with you because then it becomes self-serving. For the newspaper article, I was there when he was being interviewed by Steve Kelley of *The Seattle Times*. I just wanted to make sure that Kelley knew how much Stevie had suffered and how much he had battled.

When he was a little kid, could he play?

Oh man. He could play. I saw him when he was six years old and he could beat- he could dribble through three, four, five guys and score. I remember [laughs], we were in Marymoor Park and I was standing next to coaches on my left and Tommy was kind of right behind the coach. I was a young man at the time and a professional soccer player and I probably thought I was a big shot. Stevie is scoring goals and the coach is yelling, "Pass. Pass." So I came over his shoulder and yelled, "No, don't. Let him dribble. He's scoring." You know, I think I knew he was sick. So this was his fun time. And yes, Stevie could play. He was a good player. Then when he came to us he was a very good player. Stevie just couldn't run. He was a one and two touch player. He never tried to dribble. He always knew what he was going to do with the ball before he got it. He played the easiest pass possible. He taught a lot about playing if people paid attention because Stevie didn't give the ball away and eventually, people realized that. So, the way they do it in practice was how we'd play. Stevie was always the transition guy. We played ten on ten or twelve on eleven and Stevie was on both teams. He was always the transition guy for whatever team had the ball. And it kept him...gave him something positive in his life to run around and be around the guys. The guys treated him like any other teammate. They gave him absolutely no slack. You know, he had to be on time. He came to the early-morning training sessions. He had to put in the effort.

I remember once Tony Volpe sitting next to him at training and Stevie was struggling. He physically didn't feel good. He was exhausted and Tony Volpe just turned to him. I didn't hear it, but I heard the story later. And Tony just said, "Hey, keep you F-in head up. Keep your F-in chin up." And Stevie just got up and started playing again. I mean, this is a kid who was supposed to be dead at eighteen because his lungs made so much mucus. He could not ever get a full breath. CF is such a brutal illness. His lungs would slowly but surely get filled with puss and infection. And they'd die. They were vile when he had his transplant. I remember saying to Steve, "You know if you come to Seattle U. and play for us we're going to have to tell the team. And so, you tell me if you want to come. Then I'm going to go to the players and find out if it's acceptable." And I knew they were going to say, "Yeah, we want this kid on our team." But I also knew that we should do it the right way. So Stevie thought about it for about a week and said, "Yeah, I want to play at Seattle U." Having just seen him in the hospital, our relationship started in 2002 in a very serious way and it still is strong today even though I'm no longer his soccer coach. We're in 2009 without that soccer program. Without his experience as a student, without his experience as an athlete, I think Stevie's will to live would have been cut by eighty percent had he not played for Seattle University.

So he's gotten new lungs but now is battling cancer?[8]

Yes. So I'll just tell you that he said, "Ok, I want to come." I went to the players. We said, "Here's the situation. I'm not going to tell you guys the name because I don't know if he's coming yet or not. But would you accept it?" It was a no-brainer. It was a four minute conversation. I just said, "He'll do everything we do and when he can't do something he'll step out." And they were like, "Yeah, bring him. No big deal." What they agreed to was bringing in a great friend. What they agreed to was bringing in a great teacher. And they didn't know it and I didn't know it. But I have coached a lot by instincts, by paying attention, and by seeing opportunities. Stevie's dad actually had a good former teammate who was an assistant at a university college soccer program. Stevie's dad called that buddy, friend and former teammate and asked if they could make a spot for Stevie and they said "No." I think that's why we win national championships because we said "Yes" to

---

8. To date, Stevie has beaten his cancer and is currently pursuing a second lung transplant.

those kinds of things. So, I'm disappointed that the guy said to a teammate, "No, I can't make time- I can't make room for your son." And it wasn't even his decision because he was an assistant coach.

And Stevie's dad played in the premier league for...?

Yes, Stevie's dad played for South Hampton and back when it was English First Division, which is now the Premier League. Stevie's dad was a very good player. You know, it's brutal to see your son that way and honestly I was just talking to Tommy last night, saying how impressed I was of how his relationship with Stevie has evolved just over the last couple of days. But I watched Tommy four days ago struggle with the doctors and Stevie's situation. To stand in those conversations was pretty breathtaking really. What I think happened when Stevie came in at first, was he had to do so much to stay healthy. Seventy to eighty pills. Injections everyday. He had to have his own room. Everything had to be clean. He had to have this vest that he put on everyday for half-an-hour. It beat his chest and it beat his lungs. It put pressure on his lungs. And then it created- it loosened up the fluid and the mucus. And then he'd sit and spit for about a half-an-hour all the excess fluid that had come out of his lungs. It was absolutely gross. And when we'd go on road trips, he had to bring the machine with him.

I'll never forget when we went to San Diego. We kind of looked at what trips Stevie could go on and what trips he should go on. 'Cause going on a flight and disrupting his schedule that much was not helpful to him. But for him in his mind, it was worth the setback. So we flew to San Diego. And it was great because he was late for the airport. Mostly because his mom mistimed it. I happen to be [laughs] walking down the tunnel to the airplane. Right behind Stevie was Nick McClusky and Jason Bressler. Stevie was in the middle, McClusky was on his left and Bressler was on his right. Coach Potter and I were right behind them. And they were ripping Stevie from one side down the other for being late. They were close-talking it. And they were in his face, in his personal space. And before McClusky could finish, Bressler started in on Stevie. For fifteen-twenty minutes they let him have it. Stevie tried to refute their points and he absolutely lost that battle. Those guys were in his face [laughs]. It was great, Stevie enjoyed being called out as any regular teammate would be. It was- and there was no great humor to it. There were no humorous words spoken. They were giving Stevie a massive ration of grief for being late. And no response- mother getting there late, etc. Nothing was acceptable. It was great fun. What was great about it was that he was treated no differently than anybody else. Had he not had Cystic Fibrosis, that conversation probably wouldn't have been as intense. But because they were not going to cut him any slack, that's why it was so intense. It was great. It was 2004. I remember getting to San Diego that day and going to practice that night on the field. Stevie really had a bad session of coughing. It was very unsettling, a lot of phlegm. There were times where his coughing made me gag. I remember we were warming up in beautiful San Diego. It's at night and kind of quiet. And here's this guy coughing up, a lung, literally. I went over to him and I said, "How are you doing?" I think the changing climate, the changing altitude, the pressurization of the airplane's cabin, and whatever had really played havoc with him. Stevie just looked at me and says, "I don't know what's wrong with me. I just can't catch my breath." And I said, Steve-O, you have Cystic Fibrosis." I mean, Stevie was twenty years old and was given eighteen years to live. You know, there's a reason for it. But he couldn't understand why he was so ill. So, he often sat in the video tower with you. He was astute. He knew the game. He knew how we should play. Stevie was always on top of things. He really gave honest criticism to all the guys. But if effort wasn't put out, Stevie was extremely frustrated with that. I would ask him questions about the team, and he'd always give great insights.

And you were willing to listen?

Oh yes. Stevie always had good points. He could see it from a different set of lenses than what we could see. He would pick up different things. So yes, Stevie had valuable things to add to our coaching staff and his teammates.

Were there any moments that really stick out in your mind that could sum up his contribution to the team?

Oh yes. You know the one. I remember it clearly. In the 2004 season, we did this running exercise, which is very demanding. It started at the beginning of the year. The run is from the end line to the fifty-yard line, back to the end line and then through the fifty. So it's a hundred and seventy-two yards.

So you're doing this after a full practice?

Yes. This is the running that we do. The idea at the beginning is that we were going to do six of them and we were going to do them in groups of three. So, two guys are resting while one guy is running. The first run is to be completed in thirty-seconds. The second run is thirty-seconds. The third one is twenty-nine. The fourth one is twenty-nine. The fifth one is twenty-eight. And the sixth one is twenty-eight. So I said to the guys, "We're going to get to the place where we're going to do ten of these and we're going to have a one-to-one work to rest rate." So, one guy is running while one guy is resting. We're going to increase the number and decrease the recovery time. We're going to get there. We kept talking about it, kept paving the vision that we'd be ready when we could do ten. I didn't know this until literarily, eight months after I had left Seattle U. what actually had happened. We were saying today's the day and it was before the NCAA tournament. We had enough time to recover.

And it's darker now. Right?

Yes. Yes. It's cold. [laughs] It's wet. And it's getting dark.

Not when you want to be running.

Exactly. It's the end of practice and the guys are already tired. It's the end of the season. But I said, "Hey, today's the day we're going to do the long run. We're going to go- we're going to do ten." I said, "You're ready to do it. We've been building up this year to do ten. And you're going to do one-to-one." The first two are thirty seconds, and the last two are twenty-six seconds. In between they drop a second each time. And I'm yelling out the whole time, "Five. Six. Seven. Eight. Nine. Ten." I'm counting every second so that they can be ready and on track. Well, they didn't want to do the run. They were a bit hesitant. They lacked luster in their enthusiasm for this run. And behind me by a hundred yards was Stevie coming around the track just trying to run. He is just trying to run. Jog. You and I could walk backwards faster than Stevie was moving at that time. He's just doing everything he can to get ready for his big national championship which is getting a lung transplant. And the guys look. They see him over my right shoulder. They recognize in a pretty quick moment that their running versus his running is nothing. So they commit to do it. And they do it. We get through ten of them. And all of them do it to standard. Guys are literarily diving across the line at the last three or four. They're leaping to get across the line. And their spread -it's like they are jumping into a swimming pool to get across the line because I'm barking out, "twenty-five, twenty-six." They all had to be across by twenty-six. I know Stevie had a role in that. And then, the moment after everybody had done it, they were all flat out lying on the ground. Their chests were heaving because they were so tired. The demand had been so strong. So I just walked over and patted a lot of them on their chests and said, "Well, you're ready." And they knew it. They were ready for the NCAA tournament. At that moment we were still undefeated, and the number one ranked team in the country. But our team just went to a whole other level. The only reason why our team was able to get to an even higher level was because they saw someone who couldn't go at all. They were highly motivated by Stevie's efforts.

Pete Mullenbach, a 2004 teammate of Stevie's, shares his thoughts on Stevie's leadership impact. He shares how Stevie's presence enabled the team to stay motivated.

Another example of what our 2004 team was about and which lead to our success was the motivation provided by a member of our team who was unable to perform due to sickness. Steve Jenkins had cystic fibrosis – a deadly sickness that was actually supposed to claim his life months earlier. We prayed before every game and one of the things we always prayed for was Steve and asking God to help us to never take life or soccer for granted. Pete always did a good job of pointing out the amazing things in our lives – the fact that we had the opportunity of going to school, playing soccer, running rather than sitting behind a desk, and most of all our health. I remember one specific time in which our whole team was pissed and dreading the fact that we had to run the cooper test. Santa Maria then brought up the fact that Steve had told him how happy he would be if he was healthy enough to run this dreaded 12 minute test. He said he probably wouldn't make the time but he sure as hell would give it everything he had. I remember hearing this and thinking how lucky I was to be where I was and to be happy with what I had. You always hear about this kind of thing but it doesn't hit home unless you know someone who is sick or you yourself are sick. We all new someone who was sick and many of the older guys had played with Steve – this allowed us all to take each day like it was our last and push each other and ourselves because we knew Steve would.

One story I remember specifically during my playing days came at the end of the 2004 season, just before we headed to Texas for the finals. We were do-ing fitness, probably the hardest runs I've ever done (12 50-back-50's, the first two in 30 sec, next two in 29 and so on until the last two were to be done in 26 seconds). We did them in two groups, I was in the first group and when we finished we fell to the ground and I remember saying, 'We better f**king win this thing!' After we caught our breath everybody acknowledged this and it was almost like those in my group had a rebirth of enthusiasm and desire to perform. We did so much work up until that point to get us where we were. And especially that day I remember the training to be very difficult and fa-tiguing. Basically what I was trying to get across was the fact that we were put-ting so much work, effort and time into that season that it would be a shame for us to not win (Pete Mullenbach).

If you fast-forward, we end up winning the championship. And Stevie's health is declining quickly at that time. It's going to a new low. He's not feel-ing good but he's with us at the final four. Because he needs more treatment, he's staying with his mom and sister in a different hotel room. But he's with us. And he's not sleeping well. His sleep became much worse as time went on.

After we won the championship, the NCAA gives you watches. Well, Stevie had become ineligible at that point because he had dropped from fifteen credits to ten credits so he didn't get a watch. The redshirts didn't get watches from the NCAA right after the game. But Matt Potter, our assistant coach, who is just one of the finest human beings I know and a great competitor, just walks right up to Stevie after he got his watch hands it to him and said, "This is for you." There a lot stories, like this one that I'm telling you now that I still can't do without getting teary eyed [exhales deeply].

He got into a couple of games?

Stevie played two games his freshman year and that was awesome. Two games and it really was awesome [laughs]. He also played two games his sophomore year. I remember we were in Arizona and we put him in a game. And all the guys on the bench put their sunglasses on. Everybody is kind of teary eyed as you see this kid out there playing. After the game, a good friend, a guy I admire, Jeff Stock Sr. and I walked out of the stadium togeth-er. Stocksie was a former professional teammate of mine and he was on the trip with us. He also had played with Tommy Jenkins, Stevie's dad. Stock is a very, very successful businessman. As a soccer player, he was a hard man, a hard tackler, and a very, very good professional player. We walked out and he just said, "Stevie playing." And I responded, "Yes." We couldn't speak and that day we went to Jeff's house for dinner in Arizona, and it was the same thing. We're just sitting there in silence. He understood how important it was when Stevie got on the field. I mean, it was almost- everything took a different tone, a different importance. You know the first game he got in everybody was saying, "Get the ball to Stevie. Get the ball to Stevie." But then the coaches said, "Look, let's not make it a show. Let's just get him the ball. Don't say anything. Just get him the ball."

I remember when Stevie was able to practice, he was very much conscious of his touch. He really wanted to do the best he could. And if it failed him, he would get very upset and drop F-bombs if he wasn't doing as well as he knew he was capable of. Can you talk a little bit about how Stevie's drive permeated to the team?

Yes. Yes. Yes. Because if he didn't have a good practice, he was upset about it. If he gave the ball away too much, he was not happy. He'd get down and was not happy unless it was good quality. One time, I remember the guys yelling at him for giving the ball away too much. And no one's going to be as hard on Stevie than Stevie. And he was not happy that he'd given the ball away. So his touch was very good. He had a really nice touch. Good skills. He loved to do skill work. And like I said, he always played the simplest pass. He didn't give the ball away very much. So even though he couldn't run, the guys couldn't get the ball from him because he never let them get close enough. He did a good job of finding an opening. He'd receive the ball and then play it quickly. If he didn't play well he was his strongest critic.

His transplant process had such an impact on us. To walk with him through his thoughts, options, and procedures was humbling. I'll never forget the conversation we had in my office, which is about a ten-by-ten foot room. He was sitting down eight feet away and we were talking. At the time, he was a sophomore and said, "Well, I have to decide whether I am going to go on the transplant list or not." And I said, "Hmm... Yeah." I feel lucky for in this conversation I kept my mouth shut. I feel really lucky. I think my instincts told me to just listen. And so I remember saying, "What do you think?" And he said, "Well if I get the transplant, I will know what it's like to run. And I'll know what it's like to be a good soccer player again. But I won't live as long. If I don't get the transplant, I'll live longer but I won't know what it's like to run and play." And I did what you just did, "Hmm." Thank goodness I didn't open my mouth and say, "Well, if I were you." Because there's no way I could ever be him. So I just sat quietly. We sat there for long enough for me to go, "Wow what a conversation. It's unbelievable to be sitting in this conversation right now." My door was closed. It was quiet. And then he just said, "I want to play." At that very moment, I knew that this conversation was now even more memorable. So I said, "Well, we got to get you on the transplant list."

It took way too long to get the transplant. I think Stevie's biggest frustration and point of anger with the medical process was that they told him he would get a transplant in three to six months. He got a bike and he trained. His health was bad and he went and lifted weights five days a week. Tommy was saying that when Stevie went and lifted weights with him, he couldn't lift the weights Stevie was lifting. So he lifted weights and rode the exercise bike. Stevie did everything he could to be fit and ready for his big game which was the surgery. Well the new lungs didn't come for twenty months. And he just got worse, and worse, and worse. So what had happened was that they changed the point system. It didn't go in his favor, the new point system. So I think, nearly eighty people got transplants ahead of him. That's what I remember hearing. And he had to be in this window where you're so sick that you have to have the transplant but you are healthy enough to survive the transplant. It ended up being March 6, 2007 when he got the transplant but in February he was really ill. Really, really ill. And he ended up being hospitalized. One day he says to me, "I'm going to die in here. I won't be here in a week." But he kept fighting, obviously. He fought minute by minute.

Stevie wasn't sleeping at that time because he was so afraid to go to sleep. He was afraid that if he went to sleep, he'd die in his sleep. So beneath his eyes were big black circles. And I'd try to talk him into sleeping. I'd try coaching him into sleeping. The first thing, he closes his eyes for twenty seconds. Then his eyes would flash open. And then there was about forty-five seconds. Later, he'd fall asleep for about a minute and twenty seconds. He really just couldn't sleep. So I told him I wouldn't do anything but watch his chest rise and fall. At that point, he had seventeen percent lung capacity. He was doing what his doctors called guppy breathing - where you're just [gasps] breathing up. You're not breathing up and out. It's not in and out. So it's extremely difficult. And he was very angry. He wanted the transplant. He wanted the transplant then. But they said, "Well, we've got to get you healthy enough." So at that moment, he was too sick for the transplant. He had gone outside the window and in the wrong direction. Stevie was now outside the window of being healthy enough for a transplant. So he was very upset. But they got him back to a healthier place, where he was back inside the transplant window. They got his numbers back up with all the I-Vs. With all the medical stuff, they got him back inside the window of being ready for a transplant. I also think the fact that many of Stevie's teammates visited him kept him fighting.

Once his number came back up, we had a meeting with Dr. Mulligan on March the 5th. Mike Mulligan - there should be a book written about him. He's really got an amazing gift. We went into a meeting with him and Kathy, his nurse. We sat there and waited for Dr. Mulligan. When he walked in, it was like Superman walked into the room. He was very, very impressive. Stevie and I had scripted what we were going to say. We had scripted what we all were going to wear. I was going to wear a suit but not the national championship ring. Stevie was going to wear the national championship watch but not the ring. We weren't going to try to push it. My goal was to tell Dr. Mulligan that he had a great champion here and that if he gave Stevie new lungs, he'd be a champion for long time and a champion for lung transplants. So we had it all scripted. But, Dr. Mulligan walked right in and just said, "Hey, I see your numbers. You're next on the list. You're not going to die. You've got three or four weeks left. And I'm not going to let you die. I'm going to pick lungs that are best for you. I'm not going to give you sixty-five year old lungs. It's my call. I'll make the call. You will not die. You're going to have a good life." And it was amazing. That conversation was just really remarkable to be a part of, really impressive to be a part of that conversation. And then Dr. Mulligan said, "Your lungs are here. And your new lungs are coming. They're not coming today. And they're not coming tomorrow. They're not coming the next week. It might take a couple of weeks." He says, "But you will make it. You will live." And that night, unfortunately a young man died at the University of Oregon. He was hit by a car late at night. Stevie got the call at two in the morning while Dr. Mulligan got on a small plane to go harvest this gift. He worked through the night and returned early in the morning. Dr. Mulligan came out at 8:45 in the morning and said to Stevie's family, "If I'm out in four hours, it will have been a great success. If I'm out in eight hours, it still will be a great success. It just had to take a little longer." Dr. Mulligan came out in three and a half hours.

At that moment, we had some soccer players from Seattle U. who were there and waiting with us. Stevie's dad Tommy had gone for a walk with some of our guys, Nick McClusky and Jason Bressler. They didn't expect Dr. Mulligan out for another hour so they were just trying to kill some time. Mike Mulligan comes walking out. You got to remember that we left his office the day before at one-o-clock in the afternoon. When we were all sleeping, he was flying to Oregon to harvest the lungs and then flying back, and then doing the surgery. He had a long day to say the least, an extremely long day. So he looked whooped. I ended up meeting with BJ, Stevie's mom, and Dr. Mulligan for the post-operative meeting. I instantly realized that this meeting was a poignant moment for Stevie and his family. They had waited since 1986 for this day. Dr. Mulligan started by saying, "These are great lungs. You're going to be thrilled with these lungs. It turns out they were from a twenty-three year old male and we couldn't have asked for a better match. They were pink." And then he said, "Stevie's lungs were so bad. They were full of black puss." It wasn't just that Stevie's lungs were awful. It was amazing what Dr. Mulligan said. "Because of the puss and the scar tissue, that's why Stevie's lungs were staying open as opposed to just deflating completely." It was really powerful, very, very powerful to be in that meeting. I looked at him, [chuckles] and I called Dr. Mulligan a stud. We are about the same age and he kind of smiled and laughed. And then I said, "A lot of people were praying for you." He looked directly at me and said, "I know. It was palpable. I could feel it." So, two months of recovery and improving health after the lung transplant. And then tragically, Stevie got post-transplant lymphoma.

What I remember about that though was that the whole team was there.

Yes. I had left Seattle University and there was no requirement by any means for them to be there. It's 2007 and I had left SU in February of 2006. So in other words, it was real. It wasn't manufactured or required for them to be there for Stevie. I remember opening the elevator doors, a day after the surgery, to come visit. And directly in front of me, inside the Intensive Care Unit waiting room was a bunch of our players. They couldn't see Stevie because he was still in intensive care but they just wanted to be in the hospital with him. And even some of their girlfriends were there too. I remember walking around, shaking hands with everyone and then them saying to me, "Let Stevie know we're here." That's one of the most moving things I remember. Stevie's teammates were all just sitting in the waiting room. They were in there studying. They were just hanging out, talking, going about their business and having a good time. But they knew their teammate's in the other room. So when I went into Stevie's intensive recovery room I just rattled off, "Santa's here. And Bobby's here. And Alex is here. Santa's girlfriend is here. And Bressler's here." Stevie was in there just nodding. You know, like "Okay. Okay." Stevie's teammates couldn't get any closer than seventy-five yards. I fortunately had special uncle status and could see Stevie for them.

Yeah. What do you think Stevie taught the team if you could summarize it in a couple of sentences?

Never give up. Attitude. Your situation is never that bad. He never gave up. I think that because he handled it so well and didn't make a big deal of it. Stevie never said, "Well I've got this and you don't know what it's like to be me." The guys never had a real sense of how difficult his health-, how challenging it was because he didn't walk around and say, "Gotta do this and this and this." He's still pretty private about it. He didn't want to make it the focal point in the relationship. I think, if Stevie did pass away, I think guys would have been real reflective and said, "That guy never complained. That guy never gave up." I think he's taught all of them and us coaches a lesson on perseverance and attitude. Never quit.

Hans Esterhuizen

Can you talk a little bit about Hans - his role with the championship push and how he came to the team?

Yes. Hans is a driven guy. We recruited him out of high school. He's from Eastern Washington. He went to Pasco High and he's a big strong guy. His recruiting video is great because he's six foot two and one hundred and ninety-five pounds. Hans had Division I football scholarship offers but he loved soccer. In his soccer video, after showing clips of him playing, Hans starts talking to the camera. While he's talking, Hans takes his shirt off.

And here's this young man who looks like USC's starting free-safety. We recruited him and had a number of engaging conversations. But he ended up going to a East Coast Division I university on a full ride. He starts a lot of games there, but ends up transferring to his second school on the West Coast because his first choice was not a good fit for him. Frankly, I don't think it was challenging for him, soccer-wise. Hans goes to his second school but never really gets in the lineup. He has a nagging injury but still gets dismissed and cut in the spring. And so when I had a conversation with him, Hans was looking for a home. We went to the Ginger Lime, a little Vietnamese restaurant. We talked about life for three and a half hours. It was great. We had a great conversation because he's not only smart but very motivated. He wants to do good things in the world. I realized Hans would be a good fit for our kind of program. I thought Seattle U. would be a good place for him. What was fun was that as we talked, Hans was definitely interviewing me more than I was interviewing him. He was asking a lot of questions while squinting his eyes at me. "Ok, is this guy telling me the truth?" And understandably so...We were his third college soccer program. Like I said, Hans was a very good, very motivated student. A very strong student. Business major. And he's doing very well in the business world now. But as we walked out of the restaurant, the fun thing was he said, "You and I just talked more than I talked with my first coach. And you and I just talked more than I did with my second coach." And so, it was great-. We couldn't give him a scholarship per the NCAA rules. He had to sit out a year because you're allowed a one time transfer and this was now his second. So Hans had to sit out a year.

And when the first day of practice came, we had twenty-seven guys on the team. Twenty-eight I think. And Hans was also coming out of a hip injury. He had the hip grind surgery as I encouraged him to get. So I said to Hans, "Well maybe- because we have such high numbers, because we share the field with the women's team...You know, we got fifty-five people training on a field. It's a tight space. Maybe you ought to not train with us and join us in the winter." And Hans just snapped [chuckles]. He was so upset. And again, Hans is a big kid. We were sitting on the team bench. He's on my right and I thought he was going to head-butt me. He was furious. Hans was furious and he voiced it. And Hans scared me because he was so upset. And I said, "Ok. Ok. We'll have you play." I thought I was in trouble. I thought I had brought in a guy who was not going to be as amiable as I had thought. But he really just wanted to play. I mean, Hans was sick when he heard me say that because he'd been discarded twice before.

So he was kind of conditioned?

Yes. Yes. Yes. He was. That's exactly right. He was conditioned to being treated poorly. And he had had enough. He didn't come to our school, his third school, when he was a serious student. He was simply doing it for soccer. He knew he was going to get his academics taken care of but he wanted to be a soccer player. So I said, "Ok, no problem. You know, we'll-." He was

37

upset because in the team picture I didn't put him in the picture because we didn't have twenty-seven uniforms. He wasn't actually eligible to be in the picture because of his two-time redshirt deal. But looking back, he was the best redshirt we've ever had. He's a leader. Hans made our team significantly better. Since he's a defender, he covered Alex Chursky and Bobby McAlister. We were tougher in practice than most opponents that we faced all year. He knew his job was to make it hard on our forwards. So Hans would fight with them, and battle with them, and push them in practice. Sometimes it got to the point, [chuckles], "Hey, relax." But he made their jobs very tough which made them better players.

Hans shares his thoughts on Pete deciding to keep him on the team.

> Cut for a Second Time... Almost. Seattle University was the third school I played soccer at. I had most recently been cut from [my second] team as a result of an injury, subsequently had surgery and came back the following season to play for Pete. Prior to committing to attend SU I interviewed and visited many schools. I was 20 years old, had played at two Universities and I knew what I wanted in a soccer coach, team and university - I found all I was looking for at SU and knew it after one dinner with Pete. The agreement between Pete and I was that I would come and redshirt the 2004 season and play in 2005.
>
> When the season started we had 35 players attend the first practice. The cast was narrowed down to 32 by the 5th day of preseason. At this point I was still mending from my surgery, not completely fit and generally not at the top of my game. Pete, as any good coach would, observed my subpar performance and asked to speak with me during a scrimmage. In our conversation Pete asked how I was feeling, I gave a candid answer – that I was clearly out of shape and mending hips (where I had surgery).
>
> In the ensuing conversation, Pete very politely asked me if I would be willing to practice with the team in the spring season. His rationale that I was injured and that we had an abundance of people on the team was sound, but I failed to see the logic. I interpreted the offer to join the team again in the spring as his way of cutting me from the team and responded negatively. Pete and I agreed to address the issue the next day in his office.
>
> My compliments and greatest thanks go to Pete. Most coaches would have seen me as an excited young man with an unpredictable demeanor who would spoil their team from the sidelines. Looking back now I expect that is the call I would have made. Pete decided not to cut me, despite a very poor reaction on my behalf (Hans Esterhuizen).

So in practice he really pushed them to work hard and get better?

Yes. Yes. They had to earn it every day with him. There were also times where I had to say, "Ok, we got to get a few guys off." So I'd say, "Hey." He would volunteer to do so. I was a bit uncomfortable taking him out at times because he wanted to play so bad. But Hans would voluntarily say, "You need us off?" And I'd say, "Yeah." And then I'd look over in the corner and he's got the guys organized and doing passing, juggling, dribbling, and sprints. He's got the redshirts and he's educating the redshirts about how we did things. The NCAA doesn't allow you to have practice after the game.

If the players want to do it on their own, that's fine. So here we are during that undefeated championship season, Hans organized it after practice and games. I'd be walking off the field and there would be ten to fifteen guys training under Hans' leadership.

Who stayed after?

Redshirts and guys who didn't play enough and some of our regular guys too. Again, this was the culture of the team. Some of the guys who only played half of the game would train longer. I'll never forget, we beat Sonoma and I was helping them get pizzas after the game from a local pizza place. And I know their coach quite well. So, we're all standing there. I had already gone to my office and ordered their pizzas. Sonoma's players had already gone up to shower. So now I'm meeting their guys out front. As their pizzas are being delivered, I'm just making sure we connect the dots. I'm on one side of the street and all the Sonoma guys are on the other side of the street hanging on our field's outer fence. They are looking through it and watching many of our guys train. After crossing the street, I overhear them saying to each other, "Man, those guys just beat us and now they're training!?" And I go, "Yeah, it's good huh?" And their coach said to me, "Your team just taught us a valuable lesson." So, the credit needs to be given to the University of Portland for they used to do the same thing under Clive Charles. But Hans led all that stuff. The guys stayed after and trained. They stayed after and worked hard because of his leadership.

From a player's perspective, Anthony Sardon echoes this story that exemplifies the team's culture of everyone striving to become the best possible soccer player they could be through hard work and dedication.

> The interesting thing when looking back at the experience was that every player seemed to be connected to the same genuine energy. We really didn't care who got the credit and amazing results stemmed from that. That energy was created raised by the environment of the coaching staff whose own inclinations were higher than our own. The other teams usually observed this after we had beaten them and we were training immediately after the games with a genuine concern for improving one's self and each another. I remember talking to a Sonoma State player later and him saying that after we had beaten them that they had watched us train and run ourselves into the ground while they were eating pizza in their vans parked outside of Championship Field. He said that completely demoralized that team for the rest of the season, because not only did we beat them [but] it showed that some of the players who played didn't get enough out of the game. This demonstrated [to them] that we raised our standards [to the point] that the outcome of the game was simply not enough (Anthony Sardon).

For example, I still can remember Jeff Stock Jr., who also was a great leader and unsung hero for us, coming up to me after a game and saying, "Coach, it's my birthday today. My family wants to take me out. Is it okay if I miss post-game practice?" This was said after the game was played because Jeff was always hopeful he'd play. I said, "You know, Jeff, that's completely voluntary. It's not mandatory if you want to miss it. No problem. I don't take roll. I don't even look at that part. I'm not allowed to." And so Jeff says, "Ok. I just wanted to let you know that I wouldn't make it for that training." I said, "Ok. No problem." So Hans and Jeff Stock Jr. were great leaders. Hans was always willing to do anything we asked of him to include pre-game preparations of the field. In fact, it got to the point where we didn't even need to ask him to do things. Hans already had the young guys organized.

Hans echoes the importance of the principle "Everyone is a leader, Everyone matters" in his thoughts regarding why the team won and what it was all about.

> I can't point to the reasons why our team won. The alchemy of hard work, talent, unique personalities, luck, coaching and numerous other elements that combined to form our team is too difficult to decipher. However, I can tell you that in my opinion we lost fewer games than others (1) because key people put the team first and (2) we had a deep roster of men that worked hard to make each other better.

> The team's leaders... Andy Stromberg, Jordan Inouye, Jeremiah Doyle and Cam Weaver set a standard for others to follow. Each, in their own way, demonstrated for the rest of the team what it meant to be focused on a team victory instead of a personal achievement. These leaders, and the rest of the team, were also pushed towards this 'team-first' focus by a coaching staff that viewed our sport as something larger than a game. They approached coaching more as a process of developing men than winning a game or having a successful season. Because our coaches took a broad view of our team's goal our leaders were able to do the same. [Assistant Coaches] Frank Bartenetti and Herbie Hoffman deserve a lot of credit for ensuring that our view remained broad, and Pete did a great job communicating it to the team. For me the team was about a group of guys making each other better. It was also a family, source of pride, place to compete, somewhere to learn and where all my closest friends were (Hans Esterhuizen).

Nick McClusky

Other leaders included guys like Nick McClusky. Nick was probably the heart of our team in a number of ways. He was just a battler. He and Jason Bressler were two of the hardest working guys we had. I remember in the off-season we'd do band work training where one guy would provide resistance for the other guy who had a big band around his waist. The gap between McClusky and Bressler was like fifteen feet while the gap between everybody else was like five feet [laughs]. And the tough part was when they had to stop because the back guy would come flying forward. Then McClusky would do it for Bressler and he'd come flying forward. They were just so demanding of each other and the rest of the team.

Nick eventually became a captain for us. Nick came in and did very good things as a freshman and got some goals, big goals for us like against Gonzaga. We played him up front at the beginning because he was a very good dribbler. But as other players came in and started, Nick settled into the center midfield spot and anchored things. He was always that hard defensive guy.

I specifically remember a time when we were playing a traditionally difficult opponent. I didn't see McClusky's tackle. I was looking somewhere else but I heard it. Earlier in the game, there had been a nasty tackle from them. This opponent is always a very blue-collar and hard working team but sometimes they did some stuff that I thought was excessive. And to make this point, one time, one of their assistant coaches wrote us a letter saying that he was embarrassed by the dirty way they had played against us. So sometimes they did stuff that we didn't appreciate. Well, within five minutes of them making a dirty tackle, McClusky went into a tackle and a clump of bodies resulted. The kid who was the perpetrator of the nasty tackle against us was helped off the field. I looked at Coach Matt Potter, and said, "What happened?"

"McClusky."

And I said, "Good for Nick." You know, Nick took care of his teammates. He took care of a lot of tasks for our team. He kept guys on track. He kept guys focused. He kept the work level high. Nick always put his needs behind that of the team's. He did whatever was needed. Even after breaking his leg, Nick did not sulk one bit. Instead, he put all of his energy into cheering for his teammates during our championship play-off run.

When Nick broke his leg in the nineteenth game of our 2004 national championship run right before the play-offs, we had other guys who could step in like John Fishbaugher who was then a freshman. Losing Nick was a big blow for us but he had taught his teammates well by his daily example and mentoring. Even when he broke his leg, Nick tried to walk off the field with both bones broken. I didn't see it. I happened to look to the bench just as he put his weight on it. He went from, "My legs' broken," to, "I think, I'm okay." Nick's adrenaline had taken over. So when he put weight on his leg, he crumpled. It couldn't hold his weight and the whole crowd collectively gasped. Their gasp made me turn and look back. He was tough.

We definitely won because of Nick. He was of the guys who made sure we kept our competitive focus but also made sure that there was a lot of fun on the team. Because of McClusky, the guys always had a good time. The guys were all characters but the center of the pranks and horseplay was always Nick. You know, "There's a time and a place for everything." When it's time to work hard, McClusky was one of those guys you could always count to push it. If I said, "Jump," Nick would ask, "How high?" He was one of those old school guys.

Jordan Inouye

Can you talk a little bit about Jordan Inouye and his leadership impact?

Yes. Jordan's a fun story. I was flying to Hawaii. And we're just about to land and I was one row ahead of Patty, my wife. She was on an aisle seat and I was seated across from her. I just looked over and said, "Did I tell you that I gotta go watch a game today?" And her exact words were, "That's no problem darling." So, we went and watched this game in Hawaii.

While I'm on the sidelines, someone says, "Well, you know, the guy you gotta see is Jordan Inouye." And I said, "Which one is he?" "Well he's not playing today. He's serving a red card suspension." So I said, "Ok. So, how can we see him play?" The next day, they set up a five-on-five scrimmage thirty miles from where we were. We drove out in a white, rusted out 1980 Cadillac limousine. It was great. We called for a taxi and that's what showed up. So we pulled into this parking lot in a limo and [chuckles] my family, Patty, Ian, Nathan, and Gabrielle all got out. I go down to the field and it is in the most lush, dense forest I've ever seen. The field is a little part down below in this little valley. It was pretty funny. I was playing soccer in the Amazon. So I watched for a while and then I stepped in. And I can tell when I play with a guy, even a little more, how they read the game and all that. Jordan was a good player. Good skillful player and smart. What sold me on him was he could play and so, he passed that test. But, when we were up in the parking lot I could tell that he really wanted to be on a team that was good and also serious...He just said, "I just want to win a national championship. I gotta get off this island. I want to win a national championship." I knew he was serious about it. So when Jordan came to Seattle U. that was his focus.

Jordan's version of being recruited by Coach Pete:

> It was funny how I became a Redhawk. I'm sitting on the sideline of a game in Hawaii. I got red carded from a game the week before so I was serving my suspension. Pete flew down to Hawaii and was at this game looking at a player on the team that we were playing against. I was clueless that Pete was watching the game. A few people on the sideline started chatting about me and telling Pete he needs to see me play. Pete and I got introduced and we set up a little practice session the next morning.
>
> It's a sunny day, humid, about 85 degrees. Hawaii, go figure...I'm at the field at about 9:30am or so and in rolls this old white Cadillac limo. I was thinking, 'Who is this idiot rolling into pulling into the parking lot?' You need to understand that this field is in the middle of a jungle. I'm not exaggerating. A place called Maunawili. There is barely a field there. The parking lot holds about 10 cars. Out pops Pete from this limo with his Nike sunglasses smiling away and I just had to laugh. We played a little small sided game, picked fresh coconuts and mangos and the rest was history (Jordan Inouye).

Jordan was a little bit older and a little bit wiser than many of his teammates. He had played two years at Hawaii Pacific so he didn't have all four years of eligibility with us. I do remember that he was sort of in and out of the lineup. That's how it was for our flank players that year because we rotated them a lot. Andy Stromberg was still unable to go for a full ninety minutes even though it had been four years since he broke his leg. Andy also had stomach problems that year - something wrong with his abs. And so, Jordan was in and out.

I just remember having a one on one meeting with Jordan after our game with Humboldt State. And Jordan said, "Why am I not playing?" And I admitted to him, "You know, I'm not sure [chuckles]. I think we probably made a mistake." So we got him more playing time. But up until that time, he never was difficult. He never was a problem. Jordan just kept working hard. And I think, we acknowledged that we had definitely overlooked him a bit but at the same time we wanted more from him. And so, Jordan became part of that flank midfielder group with Stromberg, Natalie, and Jayne-Jensen. They all rotated into the midfield. But we learned much later that Jordan was a really strong leader.

In the 90's-, in between the '96 season and the '97 season the players had a team meeting. At that meeting, the 1997 players determined what was going to happen in the future. It was more of a, "We're not giving up. We are not going to lose again to Simon Frasier in '96." Tom Hardy was teary-eyed with all the seniors. He was in their face. He was poking them as he was saying, "We're not losing." It was down at the basement of the soccer house. Tom gave a Winston Churchill speech to his teammates, "This is a bunch of rubbish with which we will not put up with." He just said, "I'm not-. We're not losing anymore to Simon Frasier."

And the 2004 championship team also had a similar team meeting without any coaches which is exactly what you want. You want the ownership. So, Jordan said to his teammates, "Why don't we win every game?" And everybody kind of blew him off. He got really upset and said, "Why don't we win every game? Tell me which game we should lose?" And so, he set a mindset – the why not win every game? And when your players make that, it's very powerful. It's an expected thing if a coach says it. But when it comes from the inside and the outside, it's powerful. Jordan made it clear to his teammates that "We're not going to take a day off." And so, Jordan led by example and worked his tail off. He was very demanding of himself, very demanding of his teammates and very loyal to the team. When Jordan wasn't getting enough playing time, he didn't whine or complain about it. But when we did have a one-on-one meeting probably seven or eight games into the season, Jordan wanted to honestly know why he wasn't getting enough time. I'm pleased that I handled it the way I did. I just said, "You're right. We should be playing you more. I'll fix it."

So in interviewing the 2004 players for this book, can you talk a little bit about how Jordan's name kept popping up? Can you talk about as a leader you might think you know who key members are but in reality you might not know?

Yes. Exactly. You think the captains are doing it or you think, the goal-scorers are the big gold stars. But, Jordan Inouye was like Jeff Stock Jr. too. I think for the 2004 team, Jordan Inouye was the guy that was like, "Hey, not good enough. Let's go." We didn't see it. We didn't hear it. We didn't know about it 'till long afterwards that he was one of the standard bearers. It was a requirement that Jordan had put into their minds. I think the guys had enough belief and trust and faith in Jordan. He held them accountable to a lot of stuff. His name-, you're right, kept coming up as an informal leader who was significant to the success of the team.

For example, Bobby McAlister shares his thoughts on Jordan's leadership impact.

Another foreshadowing of the season to come was the pre-season goal setting session. As everyone went in circle and said what they expected out of the season, Jordan Inouye said that he thought we should set our goal to have an undefeated season. I remember many comments like 'Let's try to make them realistic' and 'Come on, we need to set achievable goals.' Jordan then argued with everyone in the room that this was a realistic expectation and should be on our list of goals. Who knew how right Jordan was that day at Jacob Besagno's house (Bobby McAlister).

Pat Doran echoes Bobby's thoughts on Jordan's leadership impact.

The 2004 squad was a special group and different from the talented, yet immature '02 and '03 teams. The first step towards becoming a 'great' team, as Coach Frank Bartenetti convinced us [that] was our destiny, began in the winter prior to the 2004 season. That off-season we gathered for a series of player-only meetings to lay the groundwork for the upcoming campaign by establishing team goals, expectations and rules for off-the-field conduct. In the past, our team goals were reasonable and achievable; go undefeated at home, win the league, and make the playoffs. But this team wanted more. I distinctly remember Senior Jordan Inouye lead the attitude shift by saying 'Why can't we win every single game this year?' during one of our meetings. So that became our new goal (Pat Doran).

Hans describes how Jordan led by example.

Our team loved to play. Practices were intense... and then players stayed later to get more time in. The players on the team just couldn't get enough soccer in. Jordan Inouye was by far the best example. The man would play three quarters of a soccer game and stay after a hard fought match with me, Christo and the rest of the redshirts to play some small-sided games. It is because guys like Jordan...that we had such lofty success (Hans Esterhuizen).

In the overtime game against Dowling in the NCAA semi-finals, Jordan ends up getting the game winning assist. He does the throw-in play and passes the ball back to Bobby who then hits a screamer which goes into the net. But the official game scorer actually gave credit to Alex Chursky for the game winning assist. I mentioned this to Jordan, but for him it didn't matter because he knew he did it. He also told me, it didn't matter because the team won.

Yes. Yes...Did you talk to him about it?

Yeah.

What did he say?

"It doesn't matter. I know I did it. We won."

Yes. Yes. Those are the things that make the difference.

The powerful thing for me was that Jordan didn't worry about the credit.

Yes! Yes! Yes! Yes! God bless the Hawaiian!

Summary

The stories of Stevie Jenkins, Hans Esterhuizen, Nick McClusky and Jordan Inouye, illustrate the power behind informal and exemplary leadership. Without any of these players, Coach Pete's 2004 team does not go undefeated and win a national championship. A coach who embraces, "Everyone is a Leader, Everyone Matters", fully empowers all of the team's talent. Not only does he or she recognize the power of informal leadership but continuously looks for opportunities for it to flourish. In doing so, this enables a team to develop into its fullest potential. Pete's story of Jordan Inouye illustrates a critical point in developing high performing teams. A coach may think they know the team inside and out to include its key leaders, but in reality he or she may not be fully aware of all of the team's true leaders. A coach who cultivates an environment where everyone matters guarantees that deep frustration does not occur. Such an environment enables players to have a voice and feel comfortable enough to respectfully question things like playing time. Deeply frustrated players can eventually become alienated followers who inhibit high team performance. With an everyone matters, everyone is a leader environment, the best possible team and esprit de corps is fostered because all of the team's true leaders can thrive.

Chapter 4
Every Detail Matters

Introduction

Through the stories of Alex Chursky and Bobby McAlister, Tate Miller, Timmy Depar, Ian Chursky, and Andy Stromberg, Coach Pete illustrates why a leader must pay attention to every detail including understanding one's own bias when analyzing the details. He shares that the development of a high performing team hinges on the coach being mindful of the details - how one models team commitment. An effective coach understands that he or she is always communicating to the team and therefore must model exemplary team commitment. If not, the coach is the major roadblock of his or her team from reaching its full potential. As shared by the players of both of Pete's national championship teams, the development of a high performing team hinges on the players' collective commitment to the team's success first and foremost.

Please explain why attention to detail matters.

Staying focused on the little details is something that I am a big fan of. I was always concerned with the little details, from the equipment that we used to the way the field looked. I have never had a problem setting up the field, lining the field, and making sure the grass is painted on both sides. Blades of grass have two sides so we wanted both sides of the blades painted. So you'd have to paint it one direction and then you turned around and painted it in the other direction.

Before Nike ever had soccer signs, we made signs with the Nike swoosh to make our field look professional. And Nike actually used our signs for an NAIA national championship. We sent the Nike signs we had made to Pacific Lutheran University when they hosted the national championship. Pretty funny. So all those little details make a difference - from making our athletic trainer wear soccer studs to having bathrobes for the players' post game shower. The bathrobes weren't brand new; they were used and cost five bucks. But we embroidered guys' numbers and the school's logo on them so it probably cost us ten bucks when it was all said and done. Those bathrobes were the impetus for players staying in the locker room and talking to each other after a game. But paying attention to all those little details while gathering different viewpoints definitely makes a difference.

Can you talk a little bit about the whole culture that you strived to foster, constantly evaluating how to do better?

Yes. Yes. We were always asking that question of the assistant coaches. They were fully empowered. I'll tell you what. The assistant coaches [laughs]…Billy especially 'cause he'd been around so long, would sometimes start the half-time talk 'because he'd be so upset. He'd be, "Let me talk to them." Every assistant coach had an equal voice. This helped as we were constantly looking at ways to do things better. And that included talking to the players too. "What do you think? What can we get better on? How are things going? What do you think of this? How are the guys doing?" So we were constantly evaluating, "Are we doing things right?"

For example, I used to think team dinners at my house were a great thing. And I thought, Patty and I are going through a lot of effort to bring the guys over. But we'd practice and I'd expect them to be dressed nicely to come to our house. They'd have to go shower, change, and find a ride to get to our house. I'd then talk to them for two hours. They'd get back at nine thirty to ten o' clock at night. Then they'd start studying, the night before a game. It took Ryan Sawyer, the Rhode Scholar who said to me, "We like it. We like the meals and everything. We appreciate the effort but it really messes us up." So we stopped doing team meals at our house. We started doing team meals before games which was much better for the players. So we were constantly evaluating how we can do it better.

I'd ask players as they were leaving our program as a player and joining its alumni ranks, "What do you think of this? What do you think of that? Who are the leaders on the team?" With the coaches, the conversation was, "What about the line-up?" We'd go through the line-up over and over. "What do you think of this guy? What do you think of that guy?" I probably talked to Billy on the phone before most practices. "So how do we do it better?" You know, Herb, you were the attention-to-detail guy. You would sit back and watch and listen. And then you'd throw in things that we should be doing, that we weren't paying attention to. So every coach wasn't assigned only to a certain aspect of the team but every coach took different parts of the team to specifically focus in on. We then would all get together and discuss what we were seeing and thinking. The conversation was always centered on "How can we do it better?"

Alex and Bobby

A great example of this was the play of our forwards, Bobby and Alex. In '04, they bought in, but in '03 they were not working together. They were not helping each other. Alex would be wide open and Bobby would shoot from a bad angle. It was an unwritten, uncomfortable thing going on between them. You'd see them walk off the field, and they wouldn't be talking to each other. Coach Koch was the first one to notice this and he brought it to our attention that Bobby and Alex had separate agendas. What I am real proud of is that Jeff Koch stepped up and got right in their faces after the '03 season. He told them, "You're both being selfish. You guys got to knock it off." He was furious. He took care of it. And to me, when your assistant coaches step up and know that they have the authority, know that they are right, and know that they're doing what's best for the team and then they do it, it makes my job a lot easier. I was really proud of Kocher for getting in their faces and then they changed. I'm proud of both of those guys for changing. You know, you'd see Bobby score a great goal and even though Alex was wide open, you didn't see Alex pout or vice-versa as they did in 2003.

Do you have any examples you could illustrate?

Oh sure. You know, the goal against Bakersfield where Bobby, literarily gets the ball at midfield and dribbles past everybody.

So where and when is this game?

It's the second round of the NCAA tournament and we're ahead two-nothing. It's the second half, and Bobby gets the ball six inches inside their half, just at the fifty-yard line. And he beats five guys. Two of them fall down. And, what's great is, Craig Buitrago who is on our team bench yells louder and louder "Yes! Yes!" every time Bobby beats somebody. Meanwhile, Alex the whole time is patiently waiting for the pass... Patiently waiting. Alex is getting more open because guys keep leaving him as Bobby continues to dribble. So Bobby's now got a tough angle. He easily could have chipped it across it to Alex but he was locked in. He had radar lock and hits a left footed shot from the edge of the box against Josh Wicks who's now a goalie for D.C. United. Bobby beats Josh Wicks to the right side. From the left side he scores a great goal. Alex, the whole time was wide open. He was wide open. But you just see Alex cheer for Bobby. It was a good moment.

Then there's another time where Alex is running down the field and he plays the ball to Bobby for a header against Dominguez Hills. Alex hits a beautiful first time left-footed chip over the top and Bobby comes in and heads it. So they started working for each other in 2004, the year they won the championship. Alex really became a team player. I can remember saying to Alex in 2005, my last year as coach, I said, "You know, a lot of times, you play the right ball even though you don't want to play it." He was pleased I knew he was doing the right thing.

Can you talk a little bit about the most memorable goal of the championship season? Please talk about scoring with three seconds remaining?

Yes. Yes. Well the cool thing, it's the quarterfinals and we're playing against Incarnate Word. They are a very, very good team. This is probably November 28th, 29th somewhere around there. It's the quarterfinals, a week before the national championship. And if you go back to August 26th, we played Dominguez Hills at home for our first game of the regular season. And we gave up a goal with fourteen seconds to go and Dominguez Hills tied it up to make it 2-2. So, I was pleased that we stayed on task. We didn't get upset about giving up the goal. We simply focused on the overtime. And I remember Bobby being on my left. It was one of the few times I saw his real passion. He screamed at the guys, "Come on! We've got to win!" He was fired up. About three minutes into overtime Bobby scores. He gets fouled at the edge of the box and he scores a world-class goal on a free kick. After the game, we always say, you know-, "Hey, great job." Their coach was so impressed with Bobby's goal that he wanted a copy of the video because their goalie never saw it.

After that game, we decided that we would score a goal in the last ten seconds of a game and that we weren't going to give up a goal in the last ten seconds. We were going to score a goal in the last ten seconds of a game or the last ten seconds of a half. As you know, in college soccer, they count out loud the last ten seconds. So it's clear when it's happening. So in the Bakersfield game, it was great, we had a 3-nothing win and it's the second round of the NCAA tournament. We almost score with ten seconds to go in the first-half. Here we are winning 2-nothing and Jake Besagno comes running off the field and he's fired up. He's running past me and he's saying, "Hey, we almost did it. We almost got the goal with ten seconds." All season long, we talked about scoring with ten seconds to go.

The very next game is against Incarnate Word. It's the game which will decide who goes from the West to the Final Four. In the last three minutes John Fishbaugher, a freshman, hits a great shot but Incarnate Word's goalie blocks it. We hit another shot and he blocks it again. The ball quickly goes down to our defensive end and they've got kind of an odd angle. Their guy tries to lift it, side-foot it over Jeremiah's head but he doesn't put enough weight on it. So it goes to Jeremiah who at six-five is hard to chip. Jeremiah throws it out. The ball quickly gets to Pat Doran at the edge of the box on their side. Pat goes to cross it and it gets blocked. They quickly come down our right flank in a two on one situation with thirty nine seconds to go. But Jason Cascio who is one of our starting freshmen stops it with the outside of his right foot. Cascio's form is bad for such a tackle but he's such a big, strong guy that it works. Then Jason plays it to John Fishbaugher who's about thirty-five yards out on the left side of their goal. Fishbaugher drives the ball forward to an open space for Bobby McAlister to run onto it. The ball goes over Bobby's head, but an Incarnate Word defender smartly heads it out of bounds right by our team's bench. With about fifteen seconds to go until the end of regulation, score tied o-o, Andy Stromberg comes to the line to throw it in. Andy and I are about three to four feet away from each other. I'm screaming, "Play Bobby's feet. Play Bobby's feet." And the last time, I shout as loud and hard as I can. "Play Bobby's feet!" Instinctively, Andy wants to throw it backward to Jake Besagno, who is on about the fifty so he can drive it forward. Well, Bobby's posted up at the edge of the box. Fortunately, Andy listens to me and he throws it in to Bobby. On Bobby's first touch, you hear the PA announcer say, "ten, nine, eight..." as Bobby touches the ball with the outside of his right foot back towards our goal line. Back towards our goal! He's got a guy closing in from the side and he's got a guy defending his back and a guy closing down from his front. So he's got two guys on him with a third coming. But Bobby spins the defender at his back and whips in his cross as he's falling to the ground with seven seconds. Alex Chursky who's been effectively covered all game by number three - a tall and lanky six-foot-four English guy, sprints through the box. And Alex is about fifteen yards out when he heads it. Bobby's cross has enough weight on it and it's bending away from the goal as Alex hits his diving header with five seconds to go. Alex is parallel to the ground and his head is about five feet off the ground. He's a missile as he heads it. The ball with the spin of Bobby's cross and the header from Alex takes a funny hop as it goes back towards the far post. It just bounces once and it spins under the goalie's diving reach and into the goal. I mean it's a world-class finish. World class crossing and finish. It goes in with three seconds to go. The atmosphere all that day was incredible. Around the entire field, everybody was four deep and shoulder to shoulder. And when the ball goes in, people go nuts. The beauty was that many of Incarnate Word's players started to walk off the field. They thought they were going to overtime. We didn't think we were going to overtime, we stayed on task. So we scored with three seconds to go. The splendor of all of this was Bobby unselfishly giving the ball to Alex!

Tate Miller

A great example that a coach needs to be aware of his or her own biases is Tate Miller. I've known Tate since he was a five or six years old kid. He's a six-foot-five, defender. In Tate's junior year, we were playing Western and he gives up a couple of goals. I blame him for mistakes that cost us two goals. We lose to Western. I'm upset with him and I just say to the other coaches, "He's no good. He's not going to help us. We should cut him." And Coach Frank Bartenetti says, "Yeah, you're right." Frank agrees with me and I'm surprised he agrees with me. But the reason why Frank agrees with me is because he says, "As long as you think that, that's all he's going to be able to do. If you change your thinking then Tate will be a better soccer player." And he was right.

Funny thing though, at that time I stick with my view, my story and I end up telling Tate, "You should focus completely on basketball." And Tate listens. I just don't want to see Tate Miller sit for a fourth year on the bench and not get much playing time. I don't want to torture him, knowing that he's not going to play. So the day before the first day of practice, Tate leaves me a voicemail and says, "Coach, you know, tomorrow's the first day of practice. My brother's getting married on that day. I'll be at the next day of practice after the wedding." And I smile, 'cause I know Tate's going to prove me wrong. Tate doesn't start the first game of the '97 season 'cause Tom Hardy is in there. But Tom's got a bad ankle and so Tate goes in at half time. He starts the next game and although we lost the first game of the season, we never lost after that. Tate played great. He played great all year. But I changed how I viewed Tate and Tate also proved me wrong. Players can prove you wrong.

Tate Miller '97 shares his thoughts:

> ...I was asked by Pete to leave the team winter of my junior year and told to 'focus' on my basketball career at SU because the basketball coach said I had the best jump shot on the team. The assistant soccer coach [Billy] and 7 of my teammates couldn't and didn't want to believe it. They called me every day of the week over the summer and insisted I trained with them after work for the start of pre-season. I trained with them because it helped my fitness and I liked them trying to talk me back into playing soccer my senior year. They convinced me by August and I called Pete to let him know I was 'trying out' a week before pre-season started. Of course I made the team because I'm a good player I should never have been asked to leave in the first place. I didn't start the first game of the season and we lost. I started every game the rest of the season and we never lost again. In May 2008 my teammates and I were inducted into the SU hall of fame for the school's 1st NC [national championship]. Not a bad turn of events. By the way, the basketball team won 5 games that year and I graduated before the season was over. It was the best decision of my life to play soccer at SU that year (Tate Miller).

Timmy Depar

Another good example why coaches should be aware of their own biases is Timmy Depar. His story is a fun one. Timmy is five-foot five, maybe five-four. And he played on a national championship youth team - one of two that have come out of the Northwest. He was just a great kid. Timmy was a hard worker, fearless, and would run into the goalkeeper full-speed if need be. He was a terrific team player for us.

Initially, Seattle U. was too expensive for him. Timmy comes from a pretty big family and it was just too expensive for him to go to Seattle U. So he went to a different school. Well, Timmy got cut from this school's soccer team. So, when he got cut I called him. And, here we are the national champs from the two years before - the team that beat this school often. He gets cut, and we want him at S.U. Timmy was embarrassed because he went there and didn't really communicate with me very clearly. I knew he was going there but he never really said anything about it. And he was very uncomfortable that he got cut and we still wanted him. But I saw something in Timmy. He was a fighter. He was a great team guy and he had a very strong work ethic. He was an inspirational type of kid. I didn't know if he'd start for us but I knew that he'd be a really good guy to have on the team. Plus he knew a lot of guys on our team so I thought he'd be a really good catalyst for some of those players. I thought he was mature and driven.

I also thought they had made a mistake and they had, even if you base it on one game. We were playing against them in a tight game. It's still 0-0 late in the game when Timmy Depar takes a free kick from about thirty-five yards out from the left flank. He plays it wide to his teammate, Danny Ferris. Timmy follows his kick by making a run into the box. Danny then lofts the ball into the box and Timmy, despite being five-foot four, out jumps their goalie and heads the ball in for the game winner. We win one-nothing. And that was poetic justice because this game was played at their place for the conference championship. It was great for me too because if you were to look at the hierarchy or the chain of who was stronger in that league at that time, we were probably the better team consistently year-in and year-out. I don't remember losing many times to them during those years. We were the better team for reasons like this one. They cut Timmy and we picked him up [laughs].

Ian Chursky

And the same thing happened with Ian Chursky. Like Timmy, the same opponent cut Ian and we picked him up. It's funny because I went and watched Ian Chursky play about five or six games and every time we watched him play, he'd get a goal and an assist. But, I'd call Matt Potter, our assistant coach in charge of recruiting and say, "He wasn't that good." His goals were not remarkable, just simple tap-in goals. And the next game, it was the same thing. "Well, he wasn't very good. He got two goals but they were easy goals. He just put them in." And then the next game it was, "Well Ian got a penalty kick and he scored." So he'd get a goal and two assists in the game or something. I literally had that same experience on four separate occasions. And then one day I'm walking into French Field in Kent. As I come down the stairs, Ian receives the ball at the fifty yard line, dribbles the entire way and calmly slots it for a goal. And somebody looks at me and says, "Are you getting Ian Chursky?" And I said, "Yes, he's coming to Seattle U." I offered him a scholarship in the parking lot after the game. You have to wait 'till they're outside the fence of the stadium. I apologized to Ian for being such an idiot. I just said, "I am an idiot. You know, every time I've seen you play, you've scored." However, Ian first went to a four year school and got cut by them. He then went to Tacoma Community College and scored like twenty-eight goals. And what I realized was that Ian's a goal scorer. Those guys, whether they're at a community college or whether it's the national team, if you can score goals, you can score goals. So in watching Ian play, I was looking at the process and not the results.

Ian's great and a terrific kid. He has a little different style but he's a pure, if not one of the most pure finishers we've ever had at Seattle U. But it was funny because it took me a long time to figure it out. Finally it was like, "Ok, yeah that kid's coming to Seattle U..." and so we offered him a scholarship. With Timmy Depar, we gave him $2,000. We didn't give Ian or Timmy full rides. We didn't give them half. We didn't give them twenty percent. We gave them five percent. I think we gave $5,000 to Ian. But, they knew we wanted them. So when they came, they knew that we had figured them out. They knew that we valued them and that made a big difference to them.

How did Ian perform? Any memorable goals? Any stories you can share?

Yes, sure. Yes, well one. He scored a ton of goals. I think he scored about thirty-six goals in three years for us. But he also scored big goals for us. Ian scored two goals against the University of Portland. One was a typical Ian Chursky goal. It was in overtime. It was the first time we'd ever beaten them. And the ball was played back to Portland's goal and it sort of kind of bounced around and all of the sudden Ian was in front of the goal and just passed the ball into Portland's net.

So you beat Portland at Portland?

Beat Portland at Portland.

Division One? A major program?

Yes, for us to beat the University of Portland...we had never, in my time and Clive Charles' time, had beaten them. But for us to beat them 3-2 in overtime was a huge win because we had never broken that ceiling before. We had never been able to beat Portland at Portland. That was probably the tenth time we had played them at Portland. We took that game, we hoped...we asked for that game because we wanted that experience playing on the road at a top twenty program where there's a good crowd. We wanted to make sure that we pushed ourselves. They always treated us great when we went there.

Another time I remember is playing against Sonoma State. It was over-time again and Ian Chursky did his thing. The coach at Sonoma is a good guy, Marcus Ziemer. Funny guy, he talks a lot on the sidelines and used to bait me into comments. He is one of the more enjoyable guys to coach against. Marcus is competitive as anybody but also likes to have some fun on the sidelines.

We were playing against them, in their tournament at Sonoma. We're now in sudden death overtime and just a couple of minutes in. Ian's first touch is at about the fifty. His second touch is about the thirty-five. So he's

just running full speed and goes straight to goal. And then Ian's third and final touch was at the edge of the box and then he just bends the ball around
the keeper. He slaughtered it which is why Ian was a clinical finisher. If you
gave him a chance, he'd usually put it in. The great part of that story was that
I started walking from our bench toward Marcus backing up the whole time
while Ian was taking his first, second, and third touch. And by the time, Ian
scored in sudden death overtime I was right next to Marcus. I just shook his
hand [laughs] and told him, "Good game." Marcus wasn't very happy with
me. But I knew that Ian was going to finish his chance.

And then with our big cross-town rivalry, Seattle Pacific University
(SPU); it took us ten years to beat them. Their coach is a legend. He has
won five national titles and is the second winningest coach of all time in college soccer. With Cliff McCrath, you certainly measure your program just
by beating them. Although we had already beaten them a couple of times,
there's two goals that Ian Chursky scored against SPU that were memorable. They both were game-winners. The first one came after he had a severe
broken leg against University of Portland a year earlier. He came back from
that injury where both of his right leg bones had been broken. It was not
a nasty tackle. Portland was first-class about it. Ian's leg and a defender's
leg both arrived at the ball at the same time. It was the definition of the
word crack. His leg just snapped. Ian had to come back and when he was
coming back the next season his health was unexpectedly bad. Several weeks
before the SPU game, he said, "I'm not feeling good. I've got some chest
discomfort. I'm having a hard time breathing." And Ian just got worse and
worse and worse. By the time kickoff came he could hardly walk. There was
something wrong with him. We didn't know what. We thought it was pneu-
monia at first. So he goes and takes two weeks off. He goes to the hospital
and then starts his way back. Ian's first game back is at home against SPU.
And like any rivalry game, it's a tough game. Both teams are battling and we
go into overtime with the score 2-2.

In that game, Ian played the first twenty minutes and had to come off.
He was absolutely wiped. He said, "That was too long. I can't go that long."
So we said, "Okay." So then at half time he sat, we put him back in for a little
bit, about ten minutes but he did not play much at all. And then the game
went to overtime. I vividly remember the team circle right before overtime.
I had Ian on my left. Coach Billy Collelo was to my right and he said "You
got to start Ian." And I turned to my left and said, "Ian can you go?" And
Ian went, "Uh... yes. Yes, I can go." Ian was hesitant at first and then he,
mentally just said, "I can go." And so, he went in. We scored two minutes
and fifty-four seconds in. Ian was in the right spot and put it for the game
winner. After the game, Ian was so white. We later found out that he had
a blood clot in his lungs. He was done for the whole season. Ian could have
died right on the field. He was so ill. He had a clotting disorder. Ian had to
be put on blood thinning medication which meant that he couldn't play the
remainder of the season. If Ian got hit on this medication, he could end up
internally bleeding to death. So Ian sat out that year because of the blood-

clotting problem. Prior to his clotting disorder, Ian had sat out a majority of the year with his broken leg.

The following year we were playing SPU in the first Caffe D'arte Coffee Cup at SPU. And we get a penalty kick. Nick McClusky gets taken down in the box. Again, it's overtime. So Ian goes and takes the penalty kick. And this was just a perfect way to start something like the Coffee Cup. But Ian goes to take the penalty kick and hits it soft. The ball goes right at the goalie who blocks it. The ball rebounds back out and Ian hits it again. The goalie saves it. The second time SPU's keeper hangs on to it. But while Ian was taking the kick the first time, one of the SPU players had encroached and came into the box too early. He was a good six feet in. So the referee blew the whistle before Ian hit the rebound shot. So given a second chance to re-deem himself, Ian re-took the penalty kick and kicked it with all his might into the back of SPU's net. So that was an extremely memorable goal.

Ian scored some pivotal goals for us. We beat SPU a couple of times and beat the University of Portland because of his ability to score. It's interest-ing you ask that question because he's a guy that no one else wanted. He's a guy that no one else thought would add value to the team. Ian got cut from another college team. He's one of two guys that we picked up from another school that that came in and scored key goals. Ian was very much a skilled player and a clinical finisher but it would be easy to miss the goals that he scored because they were always so seemingly easy. But the genius in Ian was his calm and composure in front of the goal. Ian could always put himself in the right spot. He also believed that he'd score every chance he got. When the referee had the penalty against SPU retaken, Bobby McAlister asked to take the penalty kick and Ian said, "No, I got it." Ian had the ball in his left hand and was putting his right hand up to hold his teammates off while say-ing, "I'm taking the kick." And then Ian got up and just buried it. He just buried it.

So looking back, – Ian's family background? Could you also talk a little bit about when he got sick and how you handled his scholarship too?

Sure. Well the cool thing for me was Ian Chursky's dad, Tony Chursky, was one of my heroes growing up just like Jeff Stock, Jimmy McAlister, Pepe Fernandez and all those guys. We had a lot of former professional play-ers' children coming through our program which I love because that meant those guys were around the program. And it was a bit of endorsement of our program having such excellent professional players now sending their kids to us.

So with Ian...I remember being Tony Chursky in my backyard as a kid. You know, playing one-on-one with my buddies. As a professional soccer player, Tony was also the players' rep for the union. So when Ian broke his leg, and then had to sit out the next year with a blood disorder, Tony called me and said, "Hey, Pete you've got to uh... you can take his scholarship. You know, we don't expect you to continue Ian's scholarship. You can use that money. You got to take care of the team first." And I appreciated that call but I told Tony right there, for me it was- those kind of issues that are real cut-and-dry. I had no problem saying, "Tony, you were there and I was there when he broke his leg. I'm not going to take his scholarship money because he did it playing for us. And his blood disorder came from the broken leg. So, until Ian graduates he gets his money." And Tony [laughs], kind of fought me on it. Which is funny because I'm saying, "No, I'm going to give you the money." And Tony's saying, "No take the money and use it for the betterment of the team." But to me, it was for the betterment of the team because we were taking care of our own people. We had a moral obligation to do that. It fit in line with the Jesuit mission statement. To me, it wasn't money lost. It was just being used by somebody...Hey, the guy broke both his leg bones. I couldn't take it. There's no way I could take Ian's scholarship. I knew that I was always sending a message to the players with my actions. How could I foster deep team commitment if I had done such a thing?

By taking care of Ian, we ended up getting Alex Chursky, his younger brother who is on our national championship team. When we all as a team stopped by the Chursky house on the way home from the University of Portland to check on Ian after his bad break, it was the right thing to do. But I also knew that we wanted Alex and his parents to know that we took care of our own. I also wanted the team to know that we took care of our own. When we stopped in, I ended up sitting in the Chursky's kitchen talking to Ian's mom, Donna and Alex. We didn't talk about Alex coming to Seattle U. We didn't talk about any of that. We just talked about Ian's injury but I knew we were sending the message to Alex. I also knew by not taking Ian's money that we were sending a message to Alex. Besides, it was the right thing to do. But it still had a value in that we never had to talk about it.

Andy Stromberg

The same thing that happened to Ian happened to Andy Stromberg. The irony with Andy was that we had changed the mascot from the Chieftains to the Redhawks and I wanted Andy to be the first Redhawk who signed a letter of intent. Andy wanted to come to Seattle U. but out of nowhere he got a full ride to the University of Richmond. And the coach was good. He gave him two weeks to decide. And Andy came back saying, "You know, that's a Division I program where we are starting up in Division II. And it's a full ride." With Andy's financial tuition, I knew it wouldn't cost us a lot. Probably six or seven thousand dollars based on his financial aid package. But, this was in November, right around Thanksgiving and we wouldn't know his financial aid package until March-April. So I said to Andy, "Will you sign a blank letter of intent? I'll guarantee you a full ride?" Again, we had done a pre-financial aid evaluation. So we knew we weren't going to go over seven thousand bucks. I said, "I'll give you a full ride but we won't know the dollar amount until March-April. Andy said, "So Coach, you want me to turn down a full ride to a Division I program to go to a Division II program with no dollar amount in place?" I said [laughs], "Yes, I guess that's what I'm saying. I want you to be the first Redhawk that signs." I continued, "You know some people that we know, the Czarnowskis. Call them up and find out if our word is good." Andy did his homework and came back and said, "I believe that you'll honor your word and so we'll do it."

The tough part on it for Andy, through his high school season- we still hadn't put a dollar amount on it. In his high school season, he had the similar both bones break that Ian Chursky did. That one was just a late tackle from a soccer player that played football and wasn't able to keep up with the pace of the game. He just came in late. But on the scholarship it said we could pull it if Andy got hurt. We hadn't really put any dollar amount to it. I could have easily have gotten out of it. But when Andy's dad Mike called... I'll never forget it. I was walking down the hallway to my office when Mike called and said "Pete, Mike Stromberg." "Mike, how are you doing?" "Uh, not good Pete. Andy broke his leg." I found out the details as I was opening my office door and getting into my desk. I then said, "Ok, give me the phone number to the hospital and I'll call Andy right now." I remember then saying, "Oh, Mike. Hey, Andy's scholarship doesn't change." And Andy's dad was really relieved. He said, "Oh, Thank God." And I started laughing. I said, "Mike, I'm going to die someday. The last thing I want is St. Peter saying to me, 'Did you really pull a scholarship from Andy Stromberg?'" The neat thing of it is that we did it because it was right thing to do.

Andy's version of what transpired with his scholarship aligns with Pete's:

I signed my commitment to attend Seattle University on February 1st, 2000. About a month later I broke my leg severely during a high school soccer game. Doctors were unsure about when I would be able to return playing – tentative dates had me out about a year but there was no definitive answer that I would ever get back to where I was before. To make matters worse, when I signed I essentially filled out a blank document. My financial aid hadn't come through yet, so I put my faith in Pete's word that he would get me the amount that we had agreed upon. Had I known the situation I was going to be in, I'm not so sure I would have been that brazen.

Pete called me in the hospital as soon as he knew about my injury. Without hesitation, he said, "Andy, I just want to let you know that nothing has changed, we're going to honor your scholarship so get well as fast as you can and you have our full support." Pete could have very easily filled in a $0 in the blank line on my pre-signed scholarship agreement. Moreover, he could have chosen not to renew my scholarship in the years that followed. It was a year and a half and 3 surgeries before I really even began my full recovery. I never got back to the level I was at when he signed me my senior year in high school. A lot of coaches would have thought better of their initial pledge and cut me loose: I simply wasn't performing to the level I should have been for the amount of money I was receiving. But Pete kept his word just because he felt it was the right thing to do.

My final season with the Redhawks was the year we won it all and I was one of the senior captains. I still didn't play all that well that season, but I smile when I think of the kind of divine justice of it all. I should have been cut, but Pete kept his word, and I ended up helping lead us to a National Championship as a result.

Maybe it would have happened without me, who knows? But I definitely think about how things turned out and it helps me to treat people well and not worry so much about immediate results. When you put people first, the results take care of themselves (Andy Stromberg).

The sad thing was that Andy never regained his full speed. He comes in his first year and he's limping. It was a bad break. Andy is a five-foot-seven, 140 pounds speedster. His game was to run up and down the flanks but he had lost his main weapon, which was his speed. So Andy limped for eighteen months. His recovery wasn't simple, or smooth, or short. But in the end, Andy ends up being elected captain of the team that wins the national championship. Alex ends up scoring the game winning-goal in the quarterfinals that gets us to the national championship. So, those guys came to Seattle U. based on a philosophy of winning national championships and great academics.

So for Alex to come to Seattle U., it was a no-brainer because he had seen how we took care of Ian. The same thing happened with Bobby McAlister. When Bobby tore his anterior cruciate ligament (ACL) for the second time in five years, his dad Jimmy called. Jimmy is another guy who was really one of my soccer heroes when I was a kid. I just love Jimmy McAlister. He says, "Take Bobby's money." And he's real blunt about it, "Take his money. He's not helping the team. Take his money." And I just fought with Jimmy saying, "No, I'm not going to take his money. He's going to stay." And then, Bobby recovers and becomes the national player of the year. If we had taken his money, it would have been unethical and we would have never won the national championship because how can you invest in the team? As a player, how can you give everything you've got to a team that pulls their scholarship money because you tore your ACL playing for that team? It doesn't work.

Summary

In the business of people, coaches need to ensure that all details are paid attention to. The stories Coach Pete provides illustrates how the difference in developing a high performing team or not hinges in being mindful of the small details and getting various perspectives on what they mean. This point is demonstrated in the story of Alex and Bobby who were purposively not working together. Coach Koch was the first to recognize this problem and bring it to the coaching staff's attention. He also addressed it because he was empowered by Coach Pete. The stories of Timmy and Ian illustrate why a coach needs to ensure that all details are paid attention especially all the intangibles a potential team member brings. Tate Miller's and Ian Chursky's stories illustrate why a coach needs to be aware of his or her own biases as they evaluate players. Lastly, Pete's stories of Andy, Ian, and Bobby demonstrate how and why a coach must model exemplary deep team commitment to his or her players. This is one critical detail that can not be ignored. As shared by Pete's 1997 and 2004 national championship players, these details foster deep team commitment that is the gateway to high performance.

Chapter 5
You Can't Save Everyone

Introduction

In this chapter, Pete shares that this principle is essential in developing a high performing team. A coach must ensure that no one is above the team. Otherwise the foundation of the team will decay and eventually crumble. While a coach needs to believe in the principle of everyone matters and is a leader, he or she must understand that you can't save everyone. There are non-negotiable behavioral expectations of being a team member. If a team member or members consistently violate the team's community, a leader must address their behavior. If not, this behavior will become the team's norm.

Can you talk a little bit about the team versus individual balancing act one must perform as a leader?

Yes, the story of Jeremiah Doyle comes to mind. I think that I err on the side of forgiveness way too much, but it's never really hurt us. We had a time when there was this goalie, Jeremiah Doyle, whom I just love. I just talked to him on Christmas and New Years and I'm so proud of him [laughs].

When Jeremiah came to us, he was a very good goalie. He joined us in 1998 and started as a freshman. When we went to final four in 1998, he was goalie of the NAIA tournament. Jeremiah is six-foot-five, very athletic and very commanding. He, to me, is the epitome of that line from Nelson Mandela: "Who are we to be fabulous, talented, and gorgeous? Who are you not to be? Your playing small does not serve God." Today, he's the kind of guy that walks into a room and spreads so much joy. You know, I love him. He also was moody, immature, and selfish back in 1998. Not a team guy. He would pout if things didn't go his way, and he would get upset. He didn't engage with the team and went home too much to Vancouver, Washington. When the team was getting together, he was gone. He was always with his girlfriend. Jeremiah was a pain since we always had to keep him happy.

In his junior year, we decided to make a change and bench him. We put in Brandon Sewell who at the time was a freshman. We were up in Vancouver, British Columbia and the benching didn't go well. Against Simon Fraser, we're down one to nothing for most of the game. Simon Frasier is such a big game for us and we found a way to tie it up with about two minutes to go. And I'll never forget it. We all were fired up except for Jeremiah. On the bench, Jeremiah had his arms crossed, his feet stretched way out and he's just staring straight ahead. The whole team is celebrating and here he is behaving like that. It just really made me sick to my stomach and very angry. So the next day at practice, Jeremiah towers over me and he says, "Am I starting against Montana?" And I said, "No, we're going to stick with Sewell." And he looks-, looms over me and says, "You think you're some kind of God." I think I've got a sense of humor, and my first response inside was, "Yeah. I am a God. Small g. I'm the god of this team and you're not playing." But had I said that [chuckles], he probably would have dropped me with a left and a right. And then, he quit the team right then and there.

And that night, I went to dinner with my lovely wife Patty, and he called a bunch of times. I just didn't answer the phone. I needed some time to think about it. Jeremiah quit the team. He wanted to come back. We had saved him a lot during that time. He had offended his teammates many times but I'd figured out ways to re-engage him. This time he offended the coaches. So the next day we talked and I just said, "No, you're not coming back. You're done." I think we had given him a good ten chances. And so, I said, "I'm not going to pull your scholarship." Because there's no point in me trying to hurt him because he's hurt us. But I could have pro-rated his scholarship to the moment he quit. I could have done it. One third for that quarter and pro-rated it right to the minute. But we didn't and that was the end of it.

Jeremiah came in June, at the end of the calendar school year and gave me a token apology. We shook hands, he went off and that was it. Three years go by and Sewell finishes his eligibility. Sewell was our starter. However, the guy behind Sewell who was going to take his spot was just not working out. We didn't cut a lot of guys from our team but there were some issues with this young fellow. He just wasn't a good fit and he had done some things to his teammates that made him not good for our team. We had given him even more chances than we gave Jeremiah. It was time for that guy to move on. So we didn't have a goalie. And here we are in March 2004, and we didn't have a goalie. I was driving to Oregon twice to look at goalkeepers and each time I had to go through Vancouver, Washington. On the way back to Seattle on the second trip, I just said, "Jeremiah Doyle. I'm going to call him up."

I knew Jeremiah's core was excellent, just some immaturity. I knew that he had some growing up to do. And so, I called him on a Tuesday. He called me back on a Wednesday. We talked for about thirty minutes. Twice he tried to apologize and I cut him off the first time. I didn't mean to, but I cut him off. The second time, when he apologized I said, "Jeremiah, can you hear me?" He said, "Yeah, I can hear you." "I forgive you." You could hear a sigh of relief. Jeremiah is a strong Christian. And he said, "Coach, you know what's crazy?" "What's that?" "I was at church on Sunday. And the preacher from New York said, 'You gotta ask for forgiveness. If you made mistakes, you gotta ask for forgiveness.'" He turned to his wife, Heidi on that Sunday and said, "I got to call Jeff and I got to call Pete." Jeff Koch is our goalie coach. Three years have gone by. That happens on a Sunday. I called him on a Tuesday. We're having a conversation on Wednesday. And I said, "That's crazy. That's unbelievable Jeremiah. You want to know why I'm calling you?" He says, "Yeah, why are you calling me?" I said, "We need a goalie. You gotta come back. If you come back we could win a national championship." And he says, "Coach, I'm married. I got a house. I got a job." And the whole time he's telling me this I'm on the other line of the phone, shaking my head, "No, No, No. No. No." He's telling me all these things and finally I say, "I don't care. I forgave you. You now owe me." So, that night we talked. He talked to his dad, Kirby. I knew that Kirby was going to be fired up about it. They tried to make it work and it did work. Jeremiah had gone back to school but he hadn't finished up. So this was his chance to come back. I knew that for one season he'd be great because he was great his freshman year. It was overtime. I knew that he'd matured. I knew that he'd relish this opportunity. I also knew he'd be good.

The fun part was that I called my assistant coaches, Matt Potter and Jeff Koch. And they're both driving East Side Catholic's soccer van when I told them, "Hey, I found a goalie." And they said, "Who?" I said, "Are you ready?" And when I told him, Coach Potter was so upset and so angry that he suggested that we bring back some other players who had had dismal histories with us. By the time I got off the phone my body language had gone from me saying, "Guess, who? Jeremiah Doyle!" to Potter and Kocher saying to me what a terrible idea it was to bring him back. My whole body language had changed. By the time we were done talking, both my elbows were on the table and my head was down.

But then Coach Koch called me thirty minutes later and said, "You know, that's a good idea." And the beauty of it was that we let a guy go 'cause it was time to let him go. We'd given him way more chances then we should have given him. I'd probably still do the same thing. But we also brought him back. And it was really beautiful. We'll have that bond forever, because, we put stuff aside for the sake of the team and the individual. You know, Jeremiah's got a son now named Finn and they're about to have another one.

When we won the national championship, CBS was filming the post-game celebration. As Jeremiah and I are walking off together, all you can hear me say is, "What did I tell you big fella?" And he goes off for five minutes about how great it was.

I told him when he came back, "You cannot have the behavior you had before. I'm going to hold you to it." One day, Jeremiah was really down and concerned about his finances. We didn't give him a big scholarship. He was trying to figure out how to make it happen. He was kind of getting a pouty face and I just looked at him and said, "You're not going to behave that way. We agreed to that." And Jeremiah just looked at me, spit in his gloves and just said really loud, "Come on. Let's go." He trotted off and got after his training. Jeremiah ends up leading us to national championship and finishing his degree. So, Jeremiah[9] is a great story, a fun one.

Summary

Pete's story of Jeremiah illustrates why a coach must ensure that no one is above the team no matter how good they are otherwise the team's foundation will eventually crumble. For these reasons, Pete had to let the self-centered Jeremiah go. If a coach does not address behavior that inhibits team development, behavior such as Jeremiah's prior to returning will become the team's norm. This principle is a counter balance to the principle of "Everyone is a Leader, Everyone Matters" for there are fundamental and non-negotiable behavioral expectations of being a team member. Fortunately for Jeremiah and Pete, this story had a happy ending largely because Pete understood that his core business as a coach is student development. In other contexts, Jeremiah may not have been allowed to make a wrong, right.

---

9. Half-way through the 2004 season, Jeremiah ended up breaking a bone in his hand which required surgery. Unbeknownst to his teammates, Jeremiah put off the surgery until the end of the season. In the end, Jeremiah became the ultimate self-less teammate.

Chapter 6
Focused Passion is the Difference

Introduction

A critical role of a coach is to keep the team both passionate and focused about what they are doing. Pete shares that this begins with who is on the team but does not end there. A prime role of an effective leader is to be watchful of the team's passion and focus at all times particularly when things are going well. This comes through in the stories shared by Coach Pete and his players.

Can you talk a little bit about the necessary burn, the passion that highly successful people possess?

Yes. Yes [chuckles]. I think that's something that every coach on our staff shared. I think many of the players came in with a passion. Bobby McAlister had a passion. Jeremiah Doyle had a passion. Alex Chursky had a passion. Cam Weaver had a passion. Jason Casio had a passion. Santa Maria had a passion. Everybody had a passion. Those are the players right off the top of my head. It's easy to list those guys. **But the whole culture became that passion. And it was the passion to do it right, to be respectful and to win.** We had won big games in 2003. We beat Gonzaga, the University of Portland, and the University of Washington all on the road. But we also lost to a lesser opponent on the road. So the passion in 2004 was to bring it for every single game. For the '97 team, it was the same. All those guys had a burning passion to play for each other.

And did you look for that in recruiting?

Yes I did. The more I recognized the value of it, the more I was willing to take a lesser skilled player who showed a fire and passion. And those guys usually rose to the standard of our play.

Can you talk a little more about more commitment and players who helped foster team commitment?

Jason Bressler

Yes, Jason Bressler comes immediately to mind. Jason is like Nick McClusky. They are sort of two peas in the pod, but Bressler just wasn't as strong a player as Nick McClusky. I remember driving to Tacoma for the annual general meeting for soccer and Bressler's mom was on the phone saying, "We've got to get this kid in. We've got to find a way for him to go to Seattle U. You know, he's from Decatur High School. They won two state championships. Alex is going and Nick is going. He's got other friends that are there. Chursky, Ian Chursky. We've got to find a way for Jason to get to Seattle U." As you know, we had to make tough decisions along the way. Honestly, he wasn't as good as others we were recruiting but we gave Bressler a seven thousand dollar scholarship, which was huge. That was a huge amount of money for us. That scholarship money is what we usually could get three or four players with, but we gave Bressler that money because he desperately wanted to be at Seattle U. He was a guy who played football. He was a very good wrestler who also played soccer and held a job. Jason had excellent grades. So when you got that combination, you say, "This guy is never going to hurt us. He's going to help us with team mentality."

Bressler was a great. You need guys on your team that are going to fill a lot of roles. He was a hard working guy who would give you everything he could at practice. As you know, I said to Jason Bressler, "I want you juggle the soccer ball five hundred times. When you juggle five hundred times let me know." It took him about eight months. But he called me one day, "Coach." I said, "Yeah?" He goes, "I just juggled five hundred times." He took it seriously and I'm glad Bressler took it seriously. I was really proud of him for doing that. He got in some games but he didn't play as much as he wanted to. His mother was more upset with me than he was. Jason knew that he had a role on the team and his role was critical. Unfortunately, he hurt his knee just before the play-offs so he couldn't do anything. But he was a role guy who everybody loved. Bressler is now in dental school at the University of Washington. He's going to be wildly successful as a dentist.

He kept the standards high of the program - the work ethic, the right kind of guy, the academic side. And we gave him a huge scholarship based on his leadership ability. I'm proud of the fact that we gave him seven grand. For example, Adam Jayne-Jensen who scored many big playoff goals for us and played much more got fifteen hundred. Some guys got a thousand dollars. But the seven grand was what was needed to get Bressler to be able to go to Seattle U. So we gave it to him. And part of it was his mom. I empathized with his mother. I also knew how bad he wanted to come. He would say, "I'm going to Seattle U. I gotta go there." You want guys on your team that want to be on your team.

Jason Bressler shares his thoughts:

> While we had a number of extremely skilled players, the so called 'piano players', the 2004 team was about blue collar hard work. Every day we were pushed by not only coaches, but by each other. Most times, our trainings were more intense than the games. We probably kicked each other harder than our opponents. This intensity was contagious and was a continuous spark for our team. Many positions on the field were constantly up for grabs which meant that any week a starter from the previous week could be replaced. With this as motivation, we were always competing with ourselves, making each other better, stronger, and fitter.
>
> For example, one day at training Pete told me that I should be able to juggle the ball 500 times without it hitting the ground. He said that he wanted me to do it before next season and to call him when I did it. Every so often I would start juggling and see how high I could get. I could always get into the 300s but never over 500. Every week, Pete would ask me if I'd done it yet and every week I'd have to tell him no. Soon I realized he was serious and expected me to really do it. Like a monkey on my back, I could never get to 500. It seemed that I would always get within 50 or so and then mess up. Finally, on a late evening in August, I juggled 756 times, called Pete, left a message on his phone, and no longer had to await the weekly, 'You juggle to 500 yet?' (Jason Bressler).

Santa Maria Rivera[10]

How about Santa Maria?

Sure. We had heard about Santa. He was playing at Walla Walla Community College. We went to the community college all-star game to see him play for the first time. We got there early so that we could watch the warm up. It was terrific because it was at Highline Community College. It was pouring down rain, and some other coaches who might be recruiting him, showed up late. Two schools in particular. We watched the warm-up. We saw what he did in warm-up. We were pleased with his skill and his effort. And then he played the first twenty minutes. In the Community College All-Star game you gotta get in as many guys in as possible. So, Santa

10. Santa went on to play for the United States Leagues (USL) Division 1 Seattle Sounders. He was on the Sounders team that won the USL Division 1 championship in 2007.

played twenty minutes and he subbed out just as the other coaches came walking up, "Anybody good?" And we said, "Nah, not really" [laughs]. And then Santa went in the second half and his team was winning. We had seen enough that we knew that we were interested in him. He didn't really do much in the second half because it was a Community College All-Star game. They hadn't been playing together. So we found him. You know, Santa's the first in his family like a lot of our guys are the first in their families to go to college.

Santa was born in Mexico and is from a pretty poor family; a family that's financially strapped. He's got to do a lot to help his family. Academically, he had to work very hard and he now has his degree, which is awesome. And that's truly an awesome thing. One day I said to him-. I'll never forget it. I was at soccer camp and we're trying to help him make sure he's eligible academically. He had signed up for a sign language class. I said, "Santa, you know you could take Spanish instead of sign language" He was quiet for a second and then said, "Sir, I would be very good at Spanish." Santa got ten credits right then and there with Spanish. Santa's like a son for me like a lot of these guys are. He was such a passionate leader. I mean he kicked the crap out of his teammates in practice which wasn't good at first, but it set a tone that that's how we trained. So practices for us, like they are for many championship teams, were truly harder than games.

So originally Santa came in as a midfielder. But the year the team wins it...?

Yes. He played sweeper. And the reason why Santa played sweeper was one of our guys didn't recover from an injury. He didn't work hard enough to get ready. It was sad and it was unfortunate. As talented as he was, he just never got himself fit enough to play. So we had to put Santa there. It's amazing when you think about it, because when Santa went and played for the Seattle Sounders, he was a midfielder. For us, he was a sweeper. It's not uncommon for somebody to go from a midfielder to a sweeper. But to go from a sweeper to a midfielder while jumping up to the next level is impressive.

Santa did a really good job for us. Again, he was a real heart and soul battler. I mean, he would kick his teammates and it became part of our culture. Santa ensured that we were going to get better even if we had to beat each other up. When we won in overtime in the semi-finals, Santa and I ended up hugging. It's embarrassing. He was sobbing. He knew we were going to win the national championship. He actually said later that when we beat Incarnate Word, he knew we'd win the championship. But we were hugging each other and jumping and spinning on the field [chuckles]. It was pretty funny. And then we fell to the ground. But he was sobbing. He was so excited. You know we've seen Santa through a lot. We'd seen Santa through some difficult scenarios with his good buddy dying, his sister serving in Iraq, etc.

You mentioned he was a real heart and soul battler. Can you say more?

Oh man, Santa's commitment. For him to get his degree, it didn't come easy. He came to us as community college guy and he played three years for us. It wasn't like three years and he was done. He had to work very, very, very hard to get his degree. But he kept at it. He stuck with it. Guys like Father Cobb helped him a lot. His teammates helped him a lot. You know, "Stay on track. Stay on task." Santa's is somebody that I'm so proud of what he's done. His commitment of doing it right over and over and over again was infectious as was his passion for soccer. Talk about the Latino passion, "Jeez Louis." He brought a lot of that to our entire team to include our coaching staff as our team captain. It was just so much fun to have him on the team. Santa also made all of us think deeper. He reminded many of us how good we have it [laughs]. You remember the day? We were driving in the van and everybody's giving him grief about something. I don't remember what and the only thing Santa could come back with was - he called us all bread-eaters. Remember that?

Yeah.

Bread-eaters... Santa did play great soccer but more importantly taught all of us about life, about privilege and the responsibilities that comes with privilege, and why we all needed to take full advantage of the opportunities we are given.

And here he was a team captain, and he said, "I'm, you know, I'm not that short from getting my degree and here I am still on the back of the bus."

Exactly [laughs]. Yes, this is where he went. There were no assigned seats. But, yes, the beauty of the program was that every guy mattered. Every guy had a role. Every guy was loved. Santa was one of the guys who made this principle a reality.

Santa Maria Rivera shares his thoughts on what was the team all about? In Santa's response, the team was all about his teammates' commitment to one another.

> When I think of my days as a Seattle University Redhawk I think of camaraderie, but when I think of the 2004 season I think of solidarity. We were unbreakable. There was no challenge that we could not meet together. We were ruthless and merciless, especially with each other. To best put it, we were the toughest opponent we played all year and we showed it day in and day out in the training field. We used to love beating the daylights out of each other and then laughing about it afterwards as we cooked dinner together later that same evening at home. It was about respect, and not just for ourselves and for our coaches, but most importantly, for our opponents. We never overlooked anybody and approached each team and each game with the outmost appreciation. It was also about responsibility. We all knew our roles and our jobs and we accepted them with great humility. When I was a kid, my grandfather used to say to me that humbleness will conquer and break the steepest and

sturdiest of barriers, and so we did, time and time again that unforgettable fall (Santa Maria Rivera).

How did you cultivate passion?

We primarily cultivated it by who we recruited. For example, Chris Hodges was a redshirt in '04. I remember him making a tackle once in a game at Curtis High School. And I just looked at Matt Potter and said, "You want to play against that?" And Coach Potter says, "No." So I said, "We're recruiting him" [chuckles]. Hodges had a passion to play. The burn was to win. The burn was to also represent properly. And the burn was to do things right. Don't leave the field a mess. Treat people with respect. Let people go ahead of you in line. The passion...All the coaches had it. Potter had it. Billy had it. You have it. Frank had it. Jeff Koch had it. You know, it all came out in different ways. There was a passion about doing right. However, there were times we as coaches had to remind and encourage them. For example, I remember once just being so furious with the guys because they weren't focusing on our set plays. I said, "Why don't I go over to my office and get the ring-sizer." I went on a tirade. And the guys didn't hear me swear very often but, on that day, I brought some tough language.

And when was that? Can you tell us the story? Who was your tirade directed towards?

Jake Besagno[11]

Oh, the whole team especially Jake Besagno [laughs]. I was so furious.

Jake. He ended up playing professional soccer for a little bit. Can you provide a little context?

Yes, Yes. Jake. Jake was a kid who again had passion. You didn't want to play against Jake. Although, he wasn't the most skillful, the most cerebral, he was a very hard guy to play against. Jake was competitive. He was an absolute battler. I wouldn't want Jake to mark me for it'd be a very lop-sided effort. Jake was an outside right back for us. He was starter all four years. We started him his freshman year. Jake's first game was at Chico State. We put him in at halftime and he started ever since then. We couldn't take him out of lineup, and we didn't think that was going to be the case. But it was Jake's work ethic and his desire on the field that was his strongest suit. He'd make mistakes but most of the time he could recover from them. But this particular time Jake was dribbling out of the back. I just went off on Jake th-

---

11.Jake went on to play for the United States Leagues (USL) Division 1 Seattle Sounders. He was on the Sounders team that won USL Division 1 championships in 2005 & 2007.

at he wasn't Franz Beckenbauer.[12] And I was just in Jake's face and said that we would name our home field, "the Jake, F-ing Besagno, F-in Beckenbauer field when we won the national championship." The guys were shocked when I gave it to him. But again, at that moment we were undefeated. We were the number one ranked team in the country. But, we still had the NCAA tournament to focus on. We weren't done and I needed to align them properly.

Bobby McAlister shares his version of Pete making sure that they stayed focused:

> Some of my favorite moments of the season had to be the training when coach (Pete) blew up on us in training. We were practicing set pieces and apparently it was not going quite as he (Coach) had envisioned it. I clearly remember running from one end-line to the other taking different angled free kicks. At some point in this process, coach brought us in and asked if we wanted him to call Josten's (the ring company) and have them start on our rings. I believe this was around mid-season, so the remark is rather funny in hindsight. The best part was it did not stop there. Coach went on to ask Jake if we should rename the field Jake Besagno field. At this, I am pretty sure the whole team was dying inside while we would never show it!! And ultimately, we would have bought a plaque which stated Jake Besagno field if we had not all been broke college students. In hindsight this was one of the funniest moments of the year (Bobby McAlister)

So you're trying to teach them a set play which actually is the one that Jordan Inouye carries out which gets the team into the national championship game. And they weren't listening?

Yes. Yes. They weren't paying attention. They all were having sidebar conversations and not focusing. And I'm working. I'm looking around saying, "You go here. I want you to do this." And as soon as I talked to one, these guys, these idiots over here started having their own conversations. I just looked around and realized no one was paying attention. So I brought them in and we had a very stern lecture. They knew I was upset. They knew I was serious. The beauty is that in the final four we scored four goals. Two of them were on set plays that hadn't worked really all year but we had put a lot of time into them and they finally paid off. One was in overtime and got us into the final. And then one was the first goal we scored in the final. Funny thing was after we won the championship, right after I gave them a speech I had planned for seven years: "Congratulations, you've joined an elite group. There are twenty-five thousand men playing college soccer this year. A hundred are going to get rings. You're one of those hundred. You're going to remember this day the rest of your life. It's going to be in your obituary. And here's what you've learned. You've learned about discipline. And you've learned about giving and receiving constructive criticism. You learned how to goal set, visualize, and self-talk. You learned how to sacri-

---

12. Franz Beckenbauer captained the German national teams to a World Cup Title in 1976 as their sweeper. He is consistently listed as one of the top eleven players in the history of professional soccer.

fice. You learned how to love. All these things apply to everything else you will do. You can be the national champion husband, the national champion father, the national championship employee, the national championship employer." When I finished the speech, they were all smiling at me. And I think it's because they are taking what I am saying to heart. But instead, Bobby McAlister raised his hand and said, "Coach, can you tell us, is it going to be renamed the Jake F-ing, Beckenbauer field?!" It was great. It was just hilarious. And I just looked at them. They were so excited to be able to throw that back at me. You know one day I'm going to sneak into that stadium and put up a little brass plaque [belly laughs]. Yes!

Alex Chursky & The Pushy Penguins

Alex Chursky shares his thoughts on how Coach Pete got his team to focus.

We took a few road trips during the fall of 2004. Before we went to the Final Four in Texas, the majority of our away matches took place all over California, with a few away fixtures in Washington and British Columbia. Being on the road could be a challenge; sometimes you didn't always have the most comfortable sleeping arrangements, there were plenty of cramped van rides, and the tap water in California tasted horrible. However, I don't think we lost sight of how lucky we were to be on these trips. If we did, Coach Pete and Coach Potter reminded us pretty quickly if we started to act ungrateful.

During these trips you get to spend a lot of down time with your teammates. It was different than being back in Seattle, where you usually spent a few hours at a time together at training or on games days. Sometimes it could be more during double-days or if there was some other team function. But on the road, you are together 24 hours a day.

This could be a mixed blessing. You get to know each other really well, but you also get to know each other too well, and it's not long before you start getting on each other's nerves. Being at a hotel together for extended periods of time, this is bound to happen. Wrestling matches often happened. Pranks happened. There were plenty of arguments. But, we were all there on a common purpose and had a great team unity. Occasionally on the road we could get out of the hotel and visit places, but apart from going to restaurants to eat most of the time in between games was spent at the hotel in our rooms.

Now, the time before games was supposed to be used for resting and eating the right food. There weren't too many problems with the food. I mean, sure guys snuck a chocolate bar in here and there, but for the most part we ate and hydrated properly.

But the resting part? A bit more challenging. To pass the time we would usually sleep, study, play cards or just watch TV. But there is only so much television you can watch or card games you can play or studying you can do before you become bored and restless.

One time in 2003, we had played a lot of cribbage in the hotels, and sometimes it got pretty competitive. Games could last for hours. One time a game extended all the way into the hotel lobby right before we left for a game against Dominguez Hills, where we subsequently got our asses kicked. We lost 3-0 and we didn't get a kick all game. Just atrocious.

One thing about our coaches is that they hated losing. That is a quality that many successful people have. And when losses occurred, they are not afraid to bring the fire and brimstone. After this particular loss, Pete just a ripped us a new one. Just really laid into us. Pete hated losing so much that he wasn't afraid to question any of the reasons why we lost. Our performance aside, one of the things he wasn't happy about was us playing too much cribbage. He had seen us in our rooms and in the lobby playing cribbage when, but to be fair to him, we really should have been more focused on the game.

I think he was just livid about the result, but during that fire and brimstone speech he hit on everything from cribbage to the soccer gods themselves. Needless to say, from then on cribbage was out. So the next year in 2004, we were on the road down in Bakersfield and we had a 7:00 p.m. kick off. This season, Jeff Stock decided to bring his Nintendo down to California so we could play some video games. I'm sure it's been done before, but because being on the road can be a bit of grind any change up in the entertainment is welcomed. So the day of the Bakersfield game there we were, myself, Stocksie, Bobby McAlister, Jake Besagno and Pat Doran just sitting around playing video games like a bunch of nerds. Sometimes when we played our stupid little video games we got pretty into the game and could start yelling at the game and each other, but we kept it down pretty quiet.

Earlier in the day, Pete had told us that he wanted us to use the time before the game to rest and to mentally prepare. We weren't really resting, but at least we were in our room and out of sight. Anyways, we had been playing this video game all afternoon and into the evening, and in this particular game we competed against each other in these types of mini-challenges, and the more you played, the more variety of challenges you could unlock. I won't go into boring details, but we wanted to unlock this stupid mini-challenge called 'Pushy Penguins' and had been trying all day to do so.

On the road, you sometimes conjure up some of the stupidest things to keep from being bored, and the importance we placed on getting that game is a little embarrassing in hindsight. But at the time, that had been our sole focus of the day. Never mind about soccer.

We had been trying for hours and were ready to give up, but decided to make one last attempt for it or else we were just going to go off and do something else. On that last try, we actually unlocked the game and all hell broke loose. We were just freaking out and jumping around yelling 'Pushy Penguins! Pushy Penguins!' Sounds dumb, I know. But you had to be there. We had been trying for so long and it finally happened.

In midst of all the commotion, we see Pete walk into the room, with all of us still in mid-celebration. We see him and he is giving us the death stare, so we quiet down quickly and put the controllers down. 'Gentleman,' Pete calmly begins, 'What... what are we supposed to be doing right now?' he asks. 'Resting,' we mumbled in unison. All of us look at him and we see his eyes are a mild shade of red, either from being woken out of a dead sleep or from a building rage. Probably a combination of both. Either way, not good.

'Right,' he said. He pointed to our television, which now had a bunch of penguins running across the screen, trampling our lifeless characters. 'This... this is not what we should be doing.' To our surprise, he calmly left the room after saying those few words. We must have been pretty loud. The rest of the team, who had been resting in their rooms, said they could hear us from way down the hall. After Pete left, we looked around at each other sort of smiling and thinking we had gotten off lightly on this one. Then it all dawned us: 'Oh shit. We better win tonight...' (Alex Chursky).

In contrast, Pete also knew when to not challenge his team's focus. This comes through in Tom Hardy's story of the how the 1997's team's practice went right before the beginning of their national tournament. The team just couldn't get anything right so Pete just called them in. All present understood that they were just full of nervous energy. All year the team had been sharp and focused so there was no sense in freaking out over a bad fifteen minute practice. Pete understood that doing so would have done more harm than good.

One of the funniest stories from the national tournament was during our final practice prior to our first game of the tournament. We usually ended practice with a crossing drill. The midfielders would make runs down the sidelines and whip in balls from the corners, where three players would run through the penalty box and usually smash crosses into the back of the net. The keepers were usually helpless, partly because there were no defenders to help them, but mostly because the shots were really easy.

Each team was given a certain amount of time on the practice field, so the next team to practice would show up and watch the last 15 minutes of the drills. So we started in on our crossing drill with next team watching us, sizing us up to see how good this unknown team from Seattle really was. The other team must have thought we were joking or goofing around because we went at least 20 or more crosses without getting one shot on target. The crosses were behind the goal and the shots were high or wide. Instead of everyone yelling and freaking out over the horrible display though, Pete just called us all in (mercifully) and we started to laugh (Tom Hardy).

In contrast to this story, Andy Stromberg shares a story of when Coach Pete had to sternly remind him and his team what they were trying to accomplish at the national tournament.

...It was the day before the national semi-final. We were bussed over to the field and were allowed to tread softly upon the grounds in our running shoes. It was all very exciting, what with the NCAA logo spray painted on the grass and the turf trimmed to perfection. We were led onto the pitch like it was holy ground; our guide stressing the fact that we needed to walk gently on the manicured blades. So, we wandered around for a few minutes and when the groundskeeper was looking the other way, I laid out a sweet practice slide tackle with no one around me. I'm still not really sure why I did it. I needed to alleviate the tension I guess. I wanted to mock our overly anal guide who treated us as though we might be some sort of grass terrorists. I did it to remind myself that I was there to have fun, even in the midst of taking the whole experience seriously and wanting to win the National Championship badly. But mostly, I just acted without thinking.

The groundskeeper didn't see me, but Pete did. He was pissed. The guys were chuckling at the absurdity of my solo slide tackle when coach pulled me aside and began scolding me. I knew he was right, but it was worth it. He was so infuriated that he tapped me gently on the cheek with his hand once as he emphasized his frustration. As I walked away one of our other captains asked me, 'Dude, did he just slap you?' 'Yup,' I replied, and went on my way smiling to myself and enjoying the freshly clipped grass (Andy Stromberg).

Summary

A highly effective coach is always mindful of his or her team's passion and focus. Through Pete's story of Jake Besagno and Alex Chursky's story of Pushy Penguins, these characteristics are not mutually exclusive. Instead, they go hand in hand. As a result, a coach needs to ensure the team is both passionate and focused about what they are doing. Pete shares that this does not end with who is picked to be on the team. It only begins. When things are going well for a team, a coach must view his or her team through the lens of focus and passion. She or he must know when to challenge the team's focus and when to back off. This balance is critical and is exemplified in how Pete reacts in the stories of Alex's Pushy Penguins, Tom Hardy's story of his team's worst practice the day before the national championship game and Andy's story about his goofy decision to slide tackle a freshly manicured field.

Chapter 7

Stay Centered on What is Important

Introduction

In this chapter, Pete describes how he used this principle to guide him in his decisions involving the team. Through the stories of how he defined winning soccer and kept his teams centered on what is important, Pete shares there are many situations that a coach of student-athletes should and must take advantage of. Authentic teachable moments occur not only on the field but also off the field. Coaches should always be looking for these authentic moments because they can inspire and bring a team closer together.

Please explain how you kept your teams centered on what is important.

You know, we fiddled around with a lot of things and tried a lot of different things but at the end of the day, the details of how we ran the program never were compromised. I think that's probably the most important thing. We made sure that we had the best schedule possible. We didn't worry about the cost, we would raise that money. I would pay for the additional cost if I had to on my own. I made sure that we had good equipment and made sure that that the behavior of the players on-and-off the field was something the school could be proud of. To me that meant the players would sit in the front third of the classroom, that they didn't wear a hat backwards. They didn't sit with their arms crossed in classes with their legs extended out, and that they were paying attention. When we were on the road, we treated all people with respect. It didn't matter who they were or what job they did. When we were on the field for practice, it was competitive. Guys were required to put out maximum effort. If we were doing the running drill for time, they had to make the time. So the standards of behavior, the standards of work, and the standards of academics were all non-negotiable. All of our coaches believed in these standards. We might have had a different way of saying it. How we trained was very important to me. And it was very, very important to all the coaches. So, staying centered on what's important included many aspects: appearance of the players, attitudes of the players, and their treatment of each other. They had to treat each other with respect. They didn't have to like each other, but they had to treat each other with respect.

Pete's Definition of Winning Soccer

I think that has to do with - obviously at the end of the day, getting the win. But along the way, allow the players to play. You've got a guy like, Bobby McAlister, a creative, attacking player. Letting him be a creative attacking player was important. We wanted him to play soccer. We wanted our outside backs to get involved as opposed to just staying home and doing nothing more than just defending. We wanted them to be part of the team's offense. We wanted them to be part of the attack. So winning soccer was skillful. It was being organized on re-starts. It was that everybody plays. There were games that we did win that weren't pretty. And that's part of winning soccer as well. There are times when you are out shot, 12 to 1 and then you score one goal and hang on. Winning soccer also is how we left the bench, how we arrived to the field. It's how we treated people at and after the game. There's more to winning the game than just walking on the field and getting the result. Staying focused on all the little details is key.

To me, winning soccer meant that once a guy joins our team, he was always with the team. The bonuses of winning soccer are when you get to go to the guys' weddings. We'd go to their parents' funerals some day. If they had children, my hope would be that we'd know those kids and perhaps even meet them at the hospital when they were born. And if they had a bank opening like Bobby McAlister's, our hope would be that we'd be there to witness it. The winning part was having a professor call me up and say his top three students in the biology department are your soccer players - Kurt Swanson, Jeremy Brown, and Shane McCorkle. So it wasn't just about wins and losses. Yes, it's great to have the wins and win a national championship by going undefeated. That's a lot of fun. But, it'd be very hollow and very temporary if the relationships weren't much deeper. If you weren't getting emails on Christmas and or text messages on Christmas and Father's Day and New Years from your past players. So the winning part was creating gentlemen. Our team rules were: Graduate. Be a gentleman. Be humble, be gracious. Don't do anything to harm your self. Treat others as you want to be treated. Be the best player and teammate you can be.

Ian Walsh

The story of how Ian Walsh came and was embraced by our team illustrates my definition of winning soccer. Ian Walsh [long pause]... I got a phone call from a buddy of mine, Joe Hunter, the coach at San Francisco State and he said, "Hey, you should look at this kid. He's a good kid. His family is going through a rough time. His dad, Owen, is very ill with cancer and it doesn't look good." We had just won the championship in '04 and we weren't look- ing for a defender. Ian came up on a visit with his mother, Gwen. Unfor- tunately we had changed the time of practice the day before. It was spring training so Ian was at practice when we weren't training. It was supposed to be a morning session. He thought we had a morning practice because I told him we had a morning practice and then we ended up moving it to the afternoon. His return flight was before the afternoon practice would have started. So he was in a tough spot because they were going to fly home. But Ian was very motivated to stay and frankly, he was at the office and I wasn't there. I got a phone call from the athletic director saying, "You got a kid here looking for you.". I came in and met with him. They were kind, gra- cious and motivated. And so they changed their flight. So Ian was able to train with us and he was okay. He was a little bit out of shape. I wouldn't say he was heavy or chunky but he was just a little bit out of shape. He prob- ably could have dropped ten pounds. But he was a big kid, six feet two and he was decent. But as I've learned - what got me was after practice. I was talking to Ian and his mom and he just flat out said, "Hey, this is where I want to go. I'll redshirt. I'll do whatever it takes." He was sincere. He really wanted to be on this team and you could tell he was a real nice young man. Good guy and he just needed a little bit of support. And in a team of twenty- seven, there's always room for somebody like that. And knowing his family situation, it just seemed like we should give him an opportunity.

That was our first interaction. Then over time we had some conversa- tions, just more detailed stuff. This is when we start. This is the training you should do in the summer. Then I had a conversation with his dad. It was a good conversation. Another conversation with Joe Hunter informed me that Ian's dad wasn't doing well. This was over about a six-month period, and about the fourth month Joe was saying, "Owen is not doing well. He might not make it." I said, "We'll find a spot for him." Having experienced losing both of my parents, I could relate and thought Ian Walsh is too young at eighteen to lose his dad. He is a twin but he is the oldest. He's got a little brother, a sister who's at Oregon State as well. Now if you fast-forward to the summer before Ian comes to train with us, we do a lot of community soccer camps and it's very busy. Our boss at that time sent out a form let- ter to all players who were sort of quote on quote, "trying out." Well in my mind, Ian wasn't really trying out but he wasn't also under a scholarship. So the form letter basically said if you get cut, you have to be out of the dorms in twenty-four hours and leave. It was a pretty cold form letter in my opinion. I had not had a lot of communication with Ian over the summer and his dad's health was getting worse. Ian and his mom showed up and they had received the letter. Gwen, Ian's mom was very nervous and a little irritated with me. I think because I hadn't been as easy to reach in the summertime, and we basically left a message saying, "Show up. We'll take care of things when you get here." For a mother who is coming from San Francisco and leaving her dying husband at home, that was not enough. And I don't blame her.

So, Gwen and Ian are there and we're doing orientation for parents and kids. When Ian goes to the orientation, Gwen kind of pulls me aside and says, "Owen is not doing well. And Ian does not know this. Owen probably has six weeks to live." We were kind of quiet for a second or two. And she started bringing up the letter that she was nervous about Ian getting cut. I remember putting my hand on her arm saying, "Gwen, your son just made the team." And she's relieved saying "Thank You." I said, "We'll keep an eye on him. We'll make sure that he get's home. You keep me posted." I made sure she had my cell phone number and said, "Give me ten days so that he gets home early, not at the last hour."

A couple of weeks later, I was driving home on the I-90 freeway and just thought, "I'm going to call Owen." I had never had a conversation with a parent like this before. It was just sort of - just seemed like the right thing to do. I happened to have Owen's phone number in my day-timer. I called him and we just had a conversation. Basically, I said to Owen that we'd take care of his kid and that was the message he got. He understood it. He got real ill, a couple of days later. Ian had been with us about eight days and I remember being aware that his father was really sick. We just went to Ian and said, "You got to go home." And he said, "No, I don't want to leave the team. This isn't a good time to leave the team." We said, "No, you have to go." It was that he really didn't have a choice as far as we were concerned. Elliot Fauske, his teammate, drove him right after one of the games. It was a pretty quick decision. Well, Owen didn't pass away then but pretty soon after. Fortunately, Ian was with him.

Ironically, our road trip to California lined up with Owen's funeral. So I flew out early on the day of the funeral. I went to the funeral. After the funeral, I went back to LAX and picked up the players. In two vanloads, we went to the reception. It was really interesting to me because we pulled in the parking lot and there were a lot of people there. It was an outdoor reception in California, in the church's courtyard. We were getting there a little bit late because of me having to leave to pick-up the guys and then come back. But I distinctly remember the twenty-five yards from the vans to the courtyard where the reception was being held. The players were very uncomfortable because they didn't really know Ian. They had spent about eight total days with him. And now here he is on their team and we're going to his dad's funeral. This was understandably so. They didn't feel they belonged. They didn't feel like they should be there - maybe they felt they were invading Ian's personal space which I think is understandable to think that. But we went in. And because we won the national championship the year before, we were sort of the defending national champs on tour. To all the people at the funeral, we were Ian's new team. When we walked in, people clapped. It was a little awkward to say the least. It wasn't a party atmosphere in our mind or theirs. But when we got in, Owens' mother, Ian's grandmother was just sobbing and giving hugs to all of our guys. Ian's mom, Gwen, was also giving everybody hugs. We went around. We ate and everybody gave Ian their condolences. It was quite powerful and we stayed until the end.

But the walk back from the courtyard to the vans, they were different guys. That was the thing that was most poignant for me. It was really poignant and so I stopped them half way or just before we got back into the vans. I looked at the guys and said, "Hey, your friends, parents are going to die. And when they do, you need to go to their funerals." And almost every guy understood the value of supporting Ian at that moment. A lot of the guys were nodding that they got it. They didn't know why the heck they were there at the beginning, but they certainly knew when they left. There's an education that comes with supporting people who have lost family members. And if you haven't experienced it, you don't know. They got a great education that day.

Jeff Koch, one of our assistant coaches was driving the other van and he said to me that the guys hardly talked. In our van, people thought, "Man, imagine losing your dad." That season, we had three guys Conner Chin, Chris Hodges, and Ian Walsh who all had parents who passed away. So, we didn't take Ian Walsh for his soccer playing. He was decent. We ended up redshirting him that season which was my last year. After I left, he continued to do very well for the guys. He became one of the team's hardest workers. We invested in the guy who had a great attitude and it paid off for the team in the long run. But most importantly, it paid off for Ian.

So I'll say this - that after the funeral, we were in this tournament and had a dinner at the Walsh's house. What was interesting for me was my phone call to Owen while I was driving down I-90 to let him know that we were going to keep an eye on his son, Ian. One of Owens' really good buddies, who spoke at Owen's funeral, came up to me after dinner at the Walsh's house and said that my call to Owen made him relax a little bit. It gave him some peace that Ian would be cared for. So, there you go...

Craig Buitrago, a member of the 2004 national championship team provides a player's perspective on this principle. He shares why a coach should continuously look for authentic teachable moments whether they are on the field or off the field. These moments can be a source of inspiration and bring the team closer together.

On particular instance that brought a true meaning of social service to our team was when we were extremely tired after a week of double days and after a hot, intense morning practice...[Pete] told us we were going to Camp Waskowitz to visit a camp for kids with multiple sclerosis (MS). We were exhausted and needed rest; however, we went there anyway to the disgruntlement of much of the team. Initially we did not know what we were doing, but only that it was an opportunity to serve others. The entire 30 minute drive from Seattle to the North Bend area was full of guys complaining or sleeping. When we arrived however, and got to experience these joy that these kids had just because we had arrived was an amazing feeling. Immediately, the feeling of exhaustion left the team and we were renewed with life and energy to interact and play with kids. I remember having races (me running) with two boys and one girl who were in electric wheel chairs. The delight and enjoyment that was experienced that afternoon was something that was used by God to change the collective heart of the team and it worked (I know it did for me, anyway). I don't remember whether we had training later that day, or if coach let us take the rest of the day off; but I do remember that was when the attitude of self-efficacy and achieving my maximum potential changed and I was a better player and teammate for it (Craig Buitrago).

Summary

A prime responsibility of a coach is keeping the team focused on its primary mission and hence its core competencies - tasks required for success. Through his stories around the definition of winning soccer and Ian Walsh, Pete illustrates that a coach of student-athletes must fundamentally understand what his or her team's mission is and what success looks like. With this understanding, a coach needs to view all team activities through this lens and evaluate if they are value added or not. An effective coach who stays centered on what is important shields his or her team from unnecessary activities while constantly searching for authentic teachable moments. Authentic teachable moments like a player's father's funeral or really engaging with less fortunate kids facilitates a student-athlete team to grow, become more inspired, and closer. This in turn results in a team that is even more resilient when it competes.

Chapter 8

Inspiring Language and Storytelling are Very Powerful Tools

Introduction

In this chapter, Pete and Coach Potter share how positive language is a very powerful tool that leaders must be consciously aware of. Deliberate positive language and legacy stories[13] can enable team members to achieve great things. The stories of Bobby McAlister, Cam Weaver, and Jason Oliver, illustrate its use by coaches must be well placed.

Can you talk a little bit about the power of inspiring language?

Bobby McAlister

When Bobby McAlister joined us from another university, he had some injuries and his ability never really came out. It didn't come to fruition. Bobby

---

13. Legacy stories were often told by alumni of the program to the current players. These stories centered on the ideas that "your career as a soccer player will be all over before you know it" and "how do you want to be remembered as a team?" In other words, "What will be your legacy?"

is a goal-scorer. He is very gifted and a dangerous player. We just had to let Bobby have freedom to play. And that wasn't a requirement that he said. It was a requirement that his dad told me about. So when he came and joined us in the first week of practice, we just said, "Ok. We want to talk to you about responsibilities you have for this team. Your expectations on the field and what we expect out of you." We said it just that way. It was kind of funny because I know it made Bobby nervous because he thought we were going to put restraints on him. I set him up to make him think that we were gonna put the reigns on him.

How did you do that?

Well, I told him about half an hour before we talked that I wanted to talk to him. During practice I said, "Hey, at the end of training I want to chat with you. I want to make sure you understand what our expectations are for you and what your role is going to be." I said it in a way that made Bobby nervous. It was all by instinct. I was having a little fun but I wanted him to be scared a little bit, a little nervous. So when everybody leaves, he comes over to Coach Billy and I who happened to be standing in the middle of the field. I said, "Look, here's the deal. You know, Bob, we're going to hold you to some things. We're going to expect certain things. And if you don't do them, it's going to hurt you and it's going to hurt the team." You could feel his tension because that's what Bobby had experienced at his last school. And so I grabbed Bobby by his right elbow and I took him into one-half of the field. I pointed to the goal and I said, "When we're going towards that goal. Your job is to score." And then I was silent. After a bit of awkward silence, Bobby said, "Ok." Then I spun him around. I grabbed Bobby and I walked to the other half. I now had a hold of Bobby's left elbow with my right hand. I said, "When you're going towards that goal in the second-half, we need you to score." It was again purposely very awkward. And Bobby said, "Ok." And I said, "That's it." And I immediately turned my back to him and started talking to Billy [laughs]. Bobby stood there for a couple of seconds, and then he says, "Thanks Coach." I said, "No problem" and he walked away.

I got a call from his dad later that day saying, "You're a genius. You just gave my kid the keys to the car." I said, "Yes, that was simple." And you know what it was? Jimmy McAlister gave me that information. Jimmy McAlister was the one - his dad. So we pulled information from wherever we needed it. He's a credible source. Jimmy[14] was a pro. Jimmy knew his kid. So why not listen to him? Jimmy was a valuable asset to us because he helped us figure his kid out. We couldn't play him as a midfielder. We couldn't play with three up front and have him underneath for that could be called

---

14. Jimmy McAlister played and starred for the Seattle Sounders back in the National American Soccer League (NASL) days. In 1977, he was NASL Rookie of the Year and also earned six caps with the U.S. nation. He currently serves as Director of Coaching for Seattle United.

a midfield position. Bobby had to be a forward. He wasn't required to defend. And you know what was interesting? Everybody knew that was his job. Sometimes, we'd poke fun at Bobby. When he did a slide tackle, we'd talk about it for a month. "Bob remember that time against Chico where you closed that guy down and you slid and you got the dirt on your shirt and your shorts?" The guys would laugh about it. We all could laugh about it because he was scoring goals. He was doing his job.

When Bobby blew out his anterior cruciate ligament for the second time-, he did it his junior year in high school and now he does it with us. I remember walking in to talk with him. I was teary-eyed and sick for him. Bobby was also teary-eyed. He knew what was ahead of him. He also knew he could come back from it but it was going to be a difficult road. So I walked up to him and just said, "Bob, we're going to get you another year of eligibility. And with that extra year we're going to get you a Master's degree. We're going to get you a national championship, and we're going to get you a wife." I was lucky that I said it for all three of those things happened. As a matter of fact, I got to preside over their wedding and it was pretty fun.

Cam Weaver

With Cam Weaver, he was an unknown. We were the only guys who recruited him. Six foot four. Two hundred and five pounds. A Handful. Hardworking. All arms, all legs, all effort. When we recruited Cam, he was a humble, hardworking, team-first kind of guy as he still is today.

One time, we were playing at Humboldt State and we were going to put him in. We tried to get him in with ten minutes to go in the half. He ended up going in with four minutes to go. But before I put him in, I just said-, and I don't even remember the conversation. Cam remembered the conversation. I said, "You're going to play in the MLS someday." I have no idea why I said that. I can't recall saying that to any other player. And he said, "Really?" I said, "Yes." He says, "Why do you say that?" "It's just where you're going to end up." So that gave him confidence. "The Dream" was an unheralded player. He was not recruited. We had actually offered a scholarship and then rescinded it because I didn't do my math properly. I originally told him it was a three thousand dollar scholarship. I met with him on a Friday night and I just had to tell him, point black, "I've got to take care of the guys who are here. I did the math wrong so I want to give you your scholarship your senior year and not your junior year. However, I'll double your scholarship. So you'll get it all your senior year." And he looked at me kind of like, "Oh my gosh, am I getting the bait and switch?" I recognized right away that Cam was nervous. I said, "Can we meet with your parents tomorrow morning?" He said, "Yeah, that'll be good."

So we met with his parents the next morning at the athletic department building before it was open. I'm thinking Cam's dad's going to beat the crap out of me or worse his mom is as I assume they are going to be upset with me [laughs]. But fortunately we sat down and they just said, "We've heard that you're honest and you'll do what's right." In the end, we ended up giving him eight grand instead of six his senior year. We gave him a thirty percent increase. But with Cam, we put him into the place where we thought he could be before he was there. We tried to do that with all our guys. Although, we still had to remind them at times, "That's not like you. That's not what this team is all about. That's not who we are."

Where is Cam today?

Well now he's, he's playing for FK Haugesund.[15] He's going to be trying out for a Bundesliga team in Germany. He went straight to the Seattle Sounders and played in the United Soccer Leagues (USL). He was the leading scorer in the league his rookie year. He tied with Romario, the great Brazilian World Cup MVP. And then he went to FK Haugesund. I feel good about what we did to help him. We helped him get a Nike contract, a really good one. That was done all over e-mail. I just said to the Nike guys, "Help this guy out. Trust me he's gonna be a good one." So he got a good deal from Nike.

Jason Oliver (J.O.)

Can you talk a little bit about Jason Oliver and his story?

Yes. That's an interesting one. Jason came to us from Indiana University. When he came to us from Indiana, Jason actually recruited us. J.O. came out and saw the school and liked our program. His first year with us, he hardly played. I didn't realize it but he only played seven minutes during the regular season. And then J.O. subbed into the final and played the last thirty minutes of the national championship game. J.O. got the assist on the game winning goal. What was great about him is I think that, because of the way we treated J.O. and because of who he was. He stayed engaged the whole time. Coach Billy Collelo (you've got to give Billy a lot of credit for this) was always encouraging J.O. during each of the three games leading up to the final. We played four games to win it. In the three games before the final, J.O. did not play.

So this is the first national championship?

First national championship '97.

In the NAIA?

Yes. We're playing Tuesday and Wednesday. Thursday is Thanksgiving so we're off. We're playing Friday afternoon in the semi-final and turning around nineteen hours later and playing in the final. The semi-final went to

---

15. Weaver is now playing for the Houston Dynamo of the MLS.

overtime and the final went to overtime. So we needed "all hands on deck." All the while, Billy kept saying to Jason throughout the tournament, "We're going to use you. You're going to get playing time. You're going to get playing time." That was Billy's terrific coaching instincts. And J.O. said, "I'm ready. I know what we do. I'm watching what they do." So when it came to sub him in, in the overtime of the national championship final, J.O. was ready. He did very well for us. I'd bet if you were to ask his teammates how much he played that year they wouldn't know. I was shocked to later learn that he only played seven minutes during the regular season in '97.

So he played seven minutes prior to the national championship game and ends up getting the game winning assist?

Yes! Yes!

So the stakes are even higher?

Oh yes, I mean, for him to go in-. We couldn't make a mistake in that game. We're knotted at 1-1 when J.O. goes in. He plays thirty minutes and then he's also gotta help us hang on for the last twelve once we scored the goal to go ahead 2-1.

And he had the game winning assist to George Czarnowski?

Yes. Yes. For J.O. to get that assist he just played a simple ball to George but it was the right ball and he was ready. It was the language. We prepared him mentally. And then, there are some players that you get closer to because they let you get closer to them or they need you to get closer to them. During his time at Seattle U., J. O. and I got very close. The next year J.O. was our starting sweeper and we went back to the final four. He did great even though he was always injured. He always had a bad back. So J.O. had to fight and do everything he could to stay healthy.

The following year, 1999, was really the worst year we ever had coaching. The reason was because we had a really bad and dysfunctional scholarship scenario. We just went back to scholarship money. Our freshman had scholarships but our sophomores, juniors and seniors didn't. And because they didn't have scholarship money our freshmen were our best players. Many of them had just come from winning a youth select national championship. Our seniors, juniors, sophomores were supposed to be the experienced leaders but they weren't. They hadn't played much. And then my dad died the day before the season. My mom had died two years before that. I was quite distant from the whole thing. And we just had some interesting characters on the team who had felt that they had peaked. They've arrived because as high school students, they won a select national championship. Fair enough, we did the same thing. It's easy to win it and think you don't need to work as hard to repeat.

But with Jason Oliver during that year, we started a youth league together. It was his idea, his vision. And I just helped and kind of made sure it could work. But that '99 season, his brother Brian passed away. He had a brain aneurism in Boston. It's one of those where he passed away before his body hit the ground. He died in the bathroom. He died instantly. And so for J.O., it was really devastating. He was doing everything he could to hold it together. He came to my house the night that his brother passed away. His family was back on the East Coast. And we'd had had some other conversations about life and doing good things. J.O. is African-American and he was trying to be a leader in his community probably earlier than his time. When J.O.'s brother passed away, it was near the end of the season. We had made the playoffs and J.O. flew back to his brother's funeral. As our team captain, J.O. then flew back to the team for the playoffs in Portland, Oregon. We were just not a good team that year. Jeremiah was our goalie and we as a group were just very dysfunctional and selfish. I'd say it was my least-engaged year coaching just because of personal stuff.

When we lost the game in Oregon, it was interesting because the crowd was honest. It was a good crowd and they were against us. They were difficult. We played most of the game with ten men due to a red card. And when we lost, Jason fell down to the ground. It was a very muddy field. We were in white uniforms and everybody's covered in mud. It was a fun game to play in if you'd won. But J.O. started sobbing and the crowd didn't pick on him. They didn't pick on us. It was as if they knew that J.O. had just lost his brother. He released all of his emotions. We were done. He had been playing for his brother. He had had something to drive for. And when we lost - there is a picture where the whole team came over to J.O.

Coach Matt Potter shares his thoughts why Seattle University's men's soccer program was successful year after year. Contained in his response is the power of telling legacy stories.

There are three main reasons, in my mind, that contributed to the success of the program- the coaching staff, 'story telling,' and the competitive spirit of the program.

Coach Fewing is a fantastic leader. He had the grand vision of what the program should be about and where it should be going. He believed in success on and off the field and spoke and thought of each constantly. He truly emphasized each equally, which is why players come away from the program with such a great appreciation for what they were a part of. Each player knew they had learned something from Coach that was more then simply X's and O's. They had learned to be good people, husbands, fathers, employees, and people.

Another vital component to the program's success was the assistant coaches. The assistant coaches during my time were foremost people of great character. They believed in the program and were selflessly dedicated to its success. They are all tough characters but we always knew they were there to help makes us better people and players. Each has unique gifts in terms of coaching and their abilities to work with people and the players. They, combined with Coach, made a tremendous coaching staff that helped form the program into what it became.

Many great cultures in our past placed high importance on the role of oral tradition/story telling to pass on and teach their culture, history, and traditions to their youth. They believed that if their youth knew about those that came before them- their greatness, achievements, the sacrifices they made, how they did things in their culture, and even their pitfalls- that they could improve upon and carry their society into the future knowing that they were a part of something larger than themselves. They would then appreciate what they had more and work harder to make their society a better place.

I believe something similar took place within the program. Stories about the program, coaches, and players have been passed down from generation to generation for as long as Coach Fewing was around. This helped create a culture where current players understood what they were a part of. They learned what the expectations were, how we acted, how we trained, and what we were about as a team. They knew of the players of the past, knew stories about them, and it helped created a unique bond between all. I am friends with guys who played in the 1980's through guys still playing there today.

These stories helped young players get to know and appreciate alumni and recognize that this program means a lot to many people and that people before them have done great things and expect great things of them. I think it helped reinforce the thought that they weren't only playing for themselves. They are playing for those who came before them, for their teammates who aren't on the field at the time, and for those who will play after their careers are done. This helped players focus, compete, and push themselves to improve. This understanding that we were a part of something bigger than ourselves created an atmosphere conducive to success- both on and off of the field.

These stories also served to teach how we do things in our program, which leads into my point about competitive spirit. There are many 'famous' stories of training sessions that have been passed down throughout the years. Each exemplifies the intensity with which we practice. Our training sessions were highly, highly competitive. The most difficult opponents we faced were ourselves. This tone was set from the first day of training camp every year. It was known that if you came to play, you would not only have to be prepared for games, but be ready to compete each and every day at training. This environment helped us to constantly improve and prepared us well for the intensity of games (Matt Potter).

Anthony Sardon echoes Coach Potter's assessment on how legacy stories impacted his teammates.

...The [powerful impact on us was] being able to connect what we learn on the field to other aspects of our lives. I think this what that coaching staff was best at. At the end of the day how we were performing as young men in life was the true measurement. Coach Pete always told us stories about past players and what they were doing know and how he could see the connection between habits and values they exhibited on the field to their career and to their family life. We heard stories about how Jason Oliver had started an urban soccer league for kids, how Ryan Sawyer was a Rhodes Scholar, and many, many other stories about successful former players. I think all of us wanted to be like the players that came before us because of what they achieved both on and off the field (Anthony Sardon).

Fastest Man Race

Legacy stories helped reinforce the expectation of winning. Humorous stories also played a role in developing "esprit de corps" within the team and around the program. Pete and his coaches looked for opportunities for these "humorous stories" to occur. As shared by Cam Mertens who was a redshirt player on the 2004 team, Coach Potter was the catalyst of this humorous story which occurred the day before the national championship game.

> My favorite memory from the national championship season was at the Final Four in Wichita Falls. I was finally healthy and able to train with the team, so it was a lot more fun for me to actually be more a part of the team than just getting gear and chasing balls. All the alumni were down in Texas for the game, including An - an alumn. I imagine they all had a good night, and maybe even a good day, of drinking in them when they came out to watch training before the semifinal game. Toward the end of practice and after the redshirts played the alumni in a game, Potter suggested that An was faster than me. I was ready to race but An didn't seem to be quite up to the challenge. All of a sudden, he tears his clothes off and is in a one piece sprinter's suit and is ready to go. We raced two times and tied but that was the first time that I really felt to be a part of the entire tradition here at Seattle U. (Cam Mertens).

It was Coach Potter who concocted the fastest man race of Cam Mertens versus An Nuon. This event is still unfortunately burned in everyone's mind's eye that was present. Those who lined the race course the morning before the national championship game included the 2004 team and many of the 1997 team members. As a show of support of the 2004 team's quest to remain undefeated and win a national championship, many members of Pete's 1997 team and their loved ones had made the trip to Wichita Falls, Texas. With a subtle go-ahead nod from Coach Potter and within seconds of both Cam and him getting into their sprinter's crouches, An removed in super-hero fashion his t-shirt that he undoubtedly had been sporting the night before and stripped down to a bottoms only Lycra running suit. All players past and present could only look on in horror. To the eyes of all gathered on each side of the race course, An's NASA wind tunnel designed speed suit had seen better days. It visibly had been stretched beyond repair. It was only a matter of time before An's speed suit was going to have a catastrophic, rubber band like failure. As An crouched into his sprinter's starting stance, many of us nervously laughed. When the first race was declared a tie and a second race to follow, this worry became even more heightened. Fortunately An's suit held together before and during the second race. The second race also ended in a tie. When a third and final race was proposed, Coach Bill Collelo decisively decided that for the greater good of all present, An and Cam's showdown speed event was finished. "Stop!!!" It was more important for An to get dressed and to call it a draw. Billy screamed at An to hurry up and get dressed. "Get out of my sight before I barf!" As the shock of what Pete's past and present players had just witnessed wore off, full belly laughter erupted into the hot Texas afternoon air.

This event was not surprising for during the 1997 team's championship run, An believed that in order for their team to win, he had to moon his teammate Craig Gauntt before each game. This act quickly became a necessary team ritual. It also had to be done in such a manner that surprised Craig. For example, before the Western regional final, An instructed Coach Pete to say a few words of inspiration as he handed out manila envelopes to all of An's teammates. Enclosed in each official looking envelope unbeknownst to Pete and An's teammates was a high definition picture of An's bottom. With the fastest man race, An was once again at the center of humorous mischief. These races cleverly conceived by An and Coach Potter helped alleviate tension the day before the national championship game. They also symbolically demonstrated the support and love that the 1997 team had for the 2004 team.

Summary

In this chapter, the stories of Bobby McAlister, Cam Weaver, Jason Oliver, and the fastest man race of Cam Mertens versus An Nuon illustrate how deliberate positive language, legacy storytelling, and humor are very powerful tools for coaches. Coaches must always consider the language they use with their team. Well placed positive language can enable team members to achieve great things they never thought possible while repeated negative language from coaches and players alike inhibits a team from achieving its full potential. Legacy storytelling can play a very powerful role by invigorating and reinforcing the team's culture of winning. Lastly, well placed humor can foster team spirit and also alleviate the stress and tension that prevent a team from performing at its best.

Conclusion

Fueled by an understanding that his players' stories on, off and most importantly after the field of play is actually his own, Peter strived to be the best leader/best coach he could be. Despite a deep rooted culture of mediocrity within the athletic department, Pete constantly strove to create an environment and culture within and around his men's soccer program that both challenged and cared for the players. Deep respect and consideration of his players on and beyond the pitch was the primary focus of Coach Fewing. Pete fundamentally understood that he was always sending a message to his players who most likely were not going to make it to the pros. Every player mattered to Pete. No one was allowed to exist on the margins whether they were a starter or a reserve player.[16]

In addition, Pete strived for an all encompassing environment where everyone involved with the men's soccer program mattered. This ranged from current to former soccer players, the team's athletic trainers and doctors, the parents of past and present players, and the assistant coaches. This mentoring[17] environment resulted in players who deeply cared and respected each other. Their commitment to each other translated into a team that

---

16. Schlossberg, Lynch, and Chickering's (1989) Mattering / Marginality Theory proposes that student success is dependent on the degree to which students feel they matter to someone else; how they are the focus of someone's attention, care and appreciation. Students who feel they do not matter and perceive to be on the margins (justified or not) are less likely to succeed.

17. An effective mentor is someone who challenges, supports, and inspires those they are mentoring (Parks Daloz, L., Keen, C., Keen, J. & Daloz Parks, S., 1996).

worked extremely hard to improve every day while forging a team resiliency that resulted in two national championships. Pete's 1997 team played four games in less than five days, playing against players from thirty-one different nations; eight players had played for their home country in World Cup qualifiers. The 1997 team won the semi-final in double overtime and nineteen hours later won the national championship in overtime. The 2004 team won their quarterfinal with three seconds remaining and scored with three minutes remaining in regulation to tie the score and force overtime. Both teams found a way to win. Talent alone was not enough. As shared by the players of both championship teams, their deep commitment to each other was the key ingredient. It enabled them to fully achieve what they were capable of.

These points come through when Pete explained why he loved coaching. Although almost all coaches want to win, notice how Pete discusses winning as a by-product of developing high school graduates into young men.

Why do you love coaching? First it's the players, the honor, and the privilege of walking with them through the 4 – 5 years, challenging them, teaching them, learning with and from them, getting to know their goals on and off and after the field and stretching them. I love the games, the locker room, the pre-game prayer, the battle, the training, watching them come in as young freshman who are so nervous on the field and not ready for the pace, contact and intensity of training. Seeing the freshman on stage at our awards banquets weighing all of 145 lbs, heads down, no eye contact, that is how they enter. Four years later they all filled out physically, but more important is their growth in confidence. They have satisfaction, direction and the comfort of being a part of a family that will last them a lifetime. They hate for it to end as do I, but they know they are welcome and expected to return as often as they can.

I love Saturday morning trainings where we start 9:00am so they can't be out late on Friday, having the players set up the drills because they know what's coming and they love all of it. [I love] the warm ups, the 3 grid game and the 7 versus 7 game to one, winner stays on, the 3 versus 2 to goal which pits goal keepers and defenders verses forwards and midfielders. It is a great way to end training the day before a game. Then a short talk and we're done by 10:15am.

Before Saturday practice I enjoy bringing our trainer, Mark Escandon two maple bars and a hot chocolate from Winchell's and delivering it to the window of his training room like Quasimodo, limping to the window and dragging my back leg, while never making eye contact and referring to him in a deep voice as 'master.' I like sending the young guys with Stevie to get my grande coffee split drip, half regular and half decaf, not so I can have a coffee as I leave the field but for them to be with Stevie and hear him breathe as he walks. They quickly realize that their sore muscle aches and bruises are actually blessings.

I love the first day of each season sorting it out with our tremendous coaches at Piecora's Pizza. I love seeing a set piece work that never worked all season then it's the winning goal in O.T. I love the love, the tough love, the 'What's going on in your life love?' or the 'Did they have your size in that shirt?' or the 'Did they sell men's clothing at the store you bought from?' or the 'We will collect some money at the end of training to pay for the other part or your hair cut.' Love the girlfriend talk, how important it is to be a gentleman, to the turning off the music that isn't appropriate in the van love. Requiring we use names of those who serve us on the road, or leaving the hotel so that those who clean up after us know we respect and appreciate their hospitality. I like putting a hand on a shoulder or a poke in the chest to emphasis how good they are and how much they are improving. The poke only works if the comments are true and positive.

I love reunions and weddings and the 'I was in the neighborhood coach', or the 'lets get lunch' or coffee reconnects. At reunions and weddings I am all smiles, there are great handshakes, eye contact and embraces that are very sincere. I like hearing about what's next, what they are doing, meeting new girlfriends who are wives to be. I love weddings. I am the fortunate pseudo proud parent. Their wives become daughters as they have become sons and as any proud parent, it is my inspiration, motivation, and joyful reward to share their stories to anyone who will listen.

On game day, a pregame meal, or road trip is another chance to learn more, preach the good news, and enjoy a great team. It's an opportunity to set the example. They understand that their coach is different and demands much of them. He holds to standards that are right. The golden rule is always to be gentlemen, be a great student, etc......

When game time comes all that has been written becomes part of the reason to win, for the team, the brotherhood, the family, the school, the alumni. It is the time to perform, to be disciplined, skillful and smart, and be a teammate. It is the time to be exhausted, to play through some pain that you thought would stop you.

I love coaching because of the other coaches who play a key role in all aspects, and with them, we work for the greater good, the different points of view that challenge the direction, that open eyes to new options that had not been thought of, all for the greater good. I love Coach Billy Colello saying 'Did you poke our captain, Kevin Houck in the chest?' and then saying 'You cannot do that, you have to apologize to him'....Billy was right and I did.

I love winning, you have to win... It's important because winning reflects upon your skill, knowledge, commitment, competitive spirit, your will, unity, expectations and standards. Winning.... everyone loves a winner. Winning provides a podium to speak of teamwork, commitment, excellence. Winning means you can say less and impact more. Winning unites schools, communities and individuals (Peter Fewing).

It's one thing for a coach to say what he or she did but more importantly it's what the players have to say about the coach once their eligibility is gone and they are free to speak the truth. Time and time again, all of Pete's players attributed the powerful impact the men's soccer program had on their lives with Pete at the helm.

Pete drove many of his former and (probably current) players bonkers. He'd say stuff like – 'If you think you can or you think you can't, you're probably right.' Or he'd say, 'Do the right things, for the right reasons.' He was relentless with his quotes and guidance about being a team of character, but more importantly he was stressing important life lessons.

Now, as I near my mid 30's, am married and have a couple kids, I eerily hear Pete's voice in my head. I'm sure as I father my children and continue my career, I'll continue to be influenced by Pete and the lessons he preached while at Seattle University (Craig Gauntt).

Championship soccer was secondary to their development. This theme resonated from players that played sparingly in games to players that won national player of the year honors. For example, Anthony Sardon, a member of

Seattle University's 2004 national championship team who played sporadically in games but always pushed his teammates to get better, shares his thoughts on the impact Coach Fewing and his staff had on his life.

> When trying to sum up my experience as a Seattle University Men's Soccer player, there are many moments that I will remember for the rest of my life. Like any player that was part of the 2004 National Championship, that was a major highlight of my playing career and will be a memory that I will take for the rest of my life. What I realized later is that I took much more away from that experience than just the title, 2004 NCAA Division II National Champion. I didn't realize at that time, but I changed drastically as a person. Certain things that seemed important no longer were. My values changed and so did my life. The one thing that Pete and our coaching staff were so brilliant at was realizing that time in our lives was a very important and formative window. I think the reason why we were so successful that season was because our focus was not on the end result, but instead on the process of achieving. That becoming a better soccer player was secondary to quest of becoming a better person in all aspects of life. This gave us great freedom to learn and to grow. We no longer looked at winning the game, but staying in the moment in order to get the best use out of that moment. We understood that if we could get the best use out of the moments then they would at up to something special (Anthony Sardon).

Andy Stromberg, a team captain of the 2004 national championship team, echoes his teammate's thoughts regarding Coach Pete's impact on his life. Developing teams that played championship soccer was a secondary focus for Pete.

> I guess if I had to sum it up in two words it would be family and excellence. Pete always strived to get us to treat us like brothers, even when it felt like you wished you weren't related to each other. For better or worse, Pete tried to help us become family, get along off the field, value relationships beyond our day to day 'soccer' interaction, and get us to build for the long term. We would often hear stories of alum getting married and being a part of each others' lives long beyond their college years. Alums would come back to practice from time to time, and coach would always give them a few minutes to share any of their advice with the team. The advice was almost always the same. 'Appreciate the time you've got here and enjoy it, because it only lasts so long.' Pete never coached anybody to say that, but it was what they all said, just the same.

> Those moments reinforced the value that what we were doing was more than just playing soccer, we were building our lives. And part of our lives were being built on the relationships we were forming on and off the field. I don't think coach would have been satisfied if we won it all but didn't have lasting relationships at the end of it. He wanted to build a family, not just a program.

> The other aspect was excellence – being excellent in your craft and being excellent in life. Pete liked to use the phrase, 'Preach the Gospel at all times. When necessary, use words.' Kind of an ironic statement coming from one of the most talkative people I've ever met. Nonetheless, I admire Coach because he always tried to do the right thing and be an excellent person in word and in deed. Intermixed with our instruction about soccer (and probably more frequently, now that I think about it), came instruction about life. After practice we were just as likely to get a lecture about how we should treat our future wives as we were to get some tips on how to cross the ball more effectively. This was kind of an ongoing point of amusement for a lot of the guys and we

would openly mock Pete from time to time for it. Pete used soccer as an analogy for life. I think his greatest joy came not from winning it all, but from seeing his players win in life. He really wanted us to be good people, not just good soccer players (Andy Stromberg).

Leadership development themes of hard work, determination, camaraderie, and resiliency come through in their stories of what they learned from their playing days. Again, playing soccer for Coach Pete and his staff was secondary to their development as future leaders.

Looking back... now that 10 years have passed, I feel like the program was preparing me and my teammates for life after soccer. The lessons that I learned from my time with the SU program were more valuable than the soccer skills that I learned. The program helped teach me to be confident in life, to deal with adversity, how to handle not always winning, to be respectful and how to treat others. I've made life-long friends from SU soccer and look at my years there as being part of something great (Tom Hardy, NAIA's men's soccer national player of the year in 1997).

Afterthoughts

We hope this collection of stories effectively demonstrate the importance of the various guiding coaching principles that fall under "Their Story is Your Story."™ These principles illustrate what authentic transformational leadership looks like in an athletic setting. To get the most out his or her team, a coach must help the players ultimately embrace the idea that their teammates' story is their story. For both national championship teams that Pete coached (1997 and 2004), they strayed from this principle the year prior and did not achieve all that they should have. This essential leadership lesson has been taken with Pete's players into their various professions. Many of Pete's former players are now in leadership positions not only in the fields of education, college and select soccer team coaches, business, health care and the military, but also as parents (see Appendix for Where Are They Now?).

We hope that this book serves as a lens for parents and their student-athletes when deciding which team and coach they should commit to and play for. For select team coaching directors and athletic directors of high schools and colleges, we hope this book serves as a model for the coaches they should be hiring and empowering. **Coaching student-athletes during their highly formative years (high school and/or college) is a moral endeavor.**

Lastly, we ask this of those who are coaching our young people, "Can you vividly tell the stories of those you are leading or have led?" For those you have coached, "Do you know how your coaching impacted them and what they are doing today?" We hope so. Their stories are your story.

Bibliography

Avolio, B. J., & Gardner, W. L. (2005). Authentic leadership development: getting to the root of positive forms of leadership. *Leadership Quarterly*, 16, 315-338.

Bass, B. M. (1985). *Leadership and performance beyond expectations*. New York: Free Press.

Bass, B. M. (1996). *A New Paradigm of Leadership: An Inquiry into Transformational Leadership Transformational leadership*. Alexandria, VA: U. S. Army Research Institute for the Behavioral and Social Sciences.

Bass, B. M. (1998a). *Transformational leadership: Industrial, military, and educational impact*. Mahwah, NJ: Erlbaum.

Bass, B. M. (1998b). *Technical Report 1104 - Transformational Leadership: Industrial, Military, and Education Impact*. Binghamton University, NY: United States Army Research Institute for the Behavioral and Social Sciences.

Bass, B. M. (2000). The future of leadership in learning organizations. *Journal of Leadership Studies*, 3, 18–41.

Bass, B. M., & Avolio, B. J. (1990). The implications of transformational and transactional leadership for individual, team, and organizational development. *Research in Organizational Change and Development*, 4, 231–272.

Bass, B. M., & Avolio, B. J. (1994). *Improving organizational effectiveness through transformational leadership*. Thousand Oaks, CA: Sage.

Bass, B. M. & Avolio, B. J. (2000). *Platoon Readiness as a Function of Leadership, Platoon, and Company Cultures. Impact*. Mahwah, NJ: Lawrence Erlbaum Associates, Publishers. Institute for the Behavioral and Social Sciences.

Brown, M. E., & Trevino, L. K. (2006). Ethical leadership: a review and future directions. *Leadership Quarterly*, 17, 595-616.

Burns, J. M. (1978). *Leadership*. New York: Harper and Row.

Coles, R. (2000). *Lives of Moral Leadership*. New York: Random House.

Collins, J. (2001). *Good to Great*. New York: HarperCollins Publishers Inc.

Collinson, D. (2006). Rethinking followership: a post-structuralist analysis of followers identities. *Leadership Quarterly*, 17, 179-189.

DeHass, D. (2009). *1981-82-2007-08 NCAA Sports Sponsorship and Participation Rates*. Indianapolis, IN. Available from: http://www.ncaapublications.com/p-3778-1981-82-2007-08-ncaa-sports-sponsorship-and-participation-rates.aspx

Dvir, T., Eden, D., Avolio, B. J., & Shamir, B. (2002). Impact of transformational leadership on follower development and performance: a field experiment. *Academy Management Journal*, 45(4), 735-744.

Dvir, T., & Shamir, B. (2003). Follower developmental characteristics as predicting transformational leadership: a longitudinal field study. *Leadership Quarterly*, 14, 327-344.

Foster, W. (1986). *The Reconstruction of Leadership*. Deakin, Victoria: Deakin University.

Fry, L. W. (2003). Toward a theory of spiritual leadership. *Leadership Quarterly*, 14, 693-727.

Gardner, J. W. (1990). *On Leadership*. New York: The Free Press.

Gardner, W. L., Avolio, B. A., Luthans, F., May, D. R., & Walumbwa, F. (2005). "Can, you see the real me?" a self-based model of authentic leader and follower development. *Leadership Quarterly*, 16, 343-372.

Graen, G. B., & Uhl-Bien, M. (1995). Development of leader-member exchange (LMX) theory of leadership over 25 years: Applying a multi-level multi-domain perspective. *Leadership Quarterly*, 6, 219–247.

Gladwell, M. (2008). *Outliers: The Story of Success*. New York: Little, Brown and Company.

Greenleaf, R. (1977). *Servant Leadership*. New York: Paulist Press.

Hoffman, H. (2010). *West Point's Impact on the Guiding Leadership Principles of its Graduates*. Saarbrucken, Germany: Lambert Academic Publishing.

Kelley, R. (1991). *The Power of Followership*. New York: Doubleday.

Machiavelli (1988). *The Prince*. Original work published 1532. Skinner, Q. & Price, R. (Eds.), Cambridge University Press: Cambridge.

McGregor, D. M. (1985). *The Human Side of Enterprise: 25th Anniversary Printing*. New York: McGraw-Hill Book Company.

Padilla, A., Hogan, R., & Kaiser, R. B. (2007). The toxic triangle: destruct-
ive leaders, susceptible followers, and conducive environments.
Leadership Quarterly, 18, 176-194.

Parks Daloz, L., Keen, C., Keen, J. & Daloz Parks, S. (1996). *Common Fire.*
Boston: Beacon-Press.

Pearce, C. L. & Conger, J. A. (Eds.), (2003). *Shared Leadership: Reframing the
Hows and Whys of Leadership.* Thousand Oaks, CA: Sage Publica-
tions, Inc.

Schriesheim, C. A., Castro, S. L., & Cogliser, C. C. (1999). Leader-member
exchange research: a comprehensive review of theory, measurement, and data-analytic practices. *Leadership Quarterly*, 10(1),
63-113.

Schlossberg, Lynch, & Chickering (1989) In L. Moore. (Ed.), *Evolving theor-
etical perspectives on students* (pp. 12-13). San Francisco: Jossey-Bass
Inc.

Sergiovanni, T. J. (1990). Adding value to leadership gets extraordinary results. *Educational Leadership*, 47, 23-27.

Smith, B. N., Montagno, R. V., & Kuzmenko, T. A. (2004). Transformational and servant leadership: content and contextual comparis-
ons. *Journal of Leadership and Organizational Studies*, 10(4), 80-91.

Tuckman, B. W. (1965). Developmental sequence in small groups. *Psycholo-
gical Bulletin, 63(6)*, 384-399.

Wang, H., Law, K. S., Hackett, R. D., Wang, D., & Cheng, Z. X., (2005).
Leader-member exchange as a mediator of the relationship
between transformational leadership and followers' performance
and organizational citizenship behavior. *Academy of Management
Journal, 48(3)*, 420-432.

Appendix – Where Are They Now?

(As of the summer of 2010)

1997 Players	Where Are They Now?
George Czarnowski	Elementary School Teacher & Youth Soccer Coach - Maple Valley, Washington
Craig Gauntt	Business Analyst, Premera Blue Cross - Shoreline, Washington
Jason Palmer	Project Manager, Environmental Consulting & Engineering Firm - Seattle, Washington
Kelly Barton	Border Patrol Agent Ajo, Arizona
Tate Miller	Medical Device Sales Representative - Seattle, Washington
Tom Hardy	City of Redmond Stream & Habitat Planner - Redmond, Washington
Tony Pyle	News & Sports Producer, Reuters - New York, New York
Jeremy Anchetta	Banking Officer - Honolulu, Hawaii
Shane McCorkle	High School Math Teacher - Missoula, Montana
Stan Thesenvitz	Middle School Teacher & Youth Soccer Coach - Burien, Washington
Arne Klubberud	Account Executive for Sogeti USA - Bellevue, Washington
An Nuon	Youth Soccer Coach for Eastside FC - Bellevue, WA
Kurt Swanson	Dentist, Barkley Village Family Dentistry - Bellingham, Washington
Jeremy Brown	Corporate Lawyer - Missoula, Montana
Sean Cassidy	Business / Real Estate Development - Kirkland, Washington
John Yamaguchi	English Teacher - Japan

Kevin Houck	Civil Engineer - Missoula, Montana
Kamal Raphael	College & Youth Soccer Coach - California
Anton Jackson	Transferred Winter Quarter, 1998 to the University of Washington
Jamin Olmstead	Business Manager, KOMO T.V. - Seattle, Washington
Jason Oliver (J.O.)	Associate Human Resources Director, AT&T Mobility - Atlanta, Georgia
Bryan Miller	Author/Writer - New York, New York
Kevin Macky	Transferred in 1998

2004 Players	Where Are They Now?
Jake Besagno	Restaurant & Construction - Seattle, Washington
Santa Maria Rivera	Information Technology & Youth Soccer Coach - Seattle, Washington
Jason Cascio	Kitsap Pumas, United Soccer Leagues - Bremerton, Washington
Eric Forner	Roofing / Caulking Company & Applying to Law School - Seattle, Washington
John Fishbaugher	Olympic Physical Therapy & Kitsap Pumas, United Soccer Leagues - Bremerton, Washington
Nick Natale	Nautilus Fitness Sales & Pursuing Masters Degree in Management - Portland, Oregon
Pat Doran	Auditor for Weyerhaeuser - Seattle, Washington
Nick McClusky	Medical Sales - Seattle, Washington
Alex Chursky	Youth Soccer Coach for Seattle United - Seattle, Washington
Bobby McAlister	Washington Federal Bank Manager & Youth Soccer Coach - Seattle, Washington
Cam Weaver	Houston Dynamo, Major League Soccer - Houston, Texas
Jordan Inouye	Senior Account Executive for BA - E-Commerce and Info. Systems - Redmond, Washington
Andy Stromberg	Puget Sound Energy & Musician - Bellingham, Washington
Luis Gamez	Bishop Blanchet High School Teacher & Youth Soccer Coach - Seattle, Washington
Chris Hodges	Expedia – Switzerland
Pete Mullenbach	Coaching Men's Soccer & Pursuing Masters Degree at Seattle University - Seattle, Washington
Cam Mertens	Pursuing Masters Degree in Sports Management at the University of San Francisco & Youth Soccer Coach - San Francisco, California
Hans Esterhuizen	Investment Analyst - Seattle, Washington
Stevie Jenkins	Authoring Book & Inspiring Others - Kent, Washington
Craig Johanson	Business Development for On-Line Advertising Company - Santa Barbara, California
Jason Bressler	University of Washington Dental School - Seattle, Washington
Jeremiah Doyle	Fish Biologist PacifiCorp Energy - Vancouver, WA

Chris Sorenson	U.S. Marines Officer - Norfolk, Virginia
Chris Natale	Sales, Pacific Office - Seattle, Washington
Adam Jayne-Jensen	University of Washington Medical School - Seattle, Washington
Christo Barker	Equity Analyst for Fisher Investments - San Francisco, California
Jeff Stock Jr.	Elementary School Teacher & Girls High School Soccer Coach - Fife, Washington
Anthony Sardon	Assistant Men's Soccer Coach, Seattle University - Seattle, Washington
Craig Buitrago	Water Resources Engineer, Parametrix, Inc. - Seattle, Washington
Justin Miller	Medical Sales - Seattle, Washington

The End / Beginning

Index

Biographies

Peter Fewing, Coach

From 1988 through 2006, Fewing served with distinction as the head men's soccer coach for Seattle University. In 1997 and 2004, his men's soccer teams won national championships which transformed Seattle University's athletic department. His 1997 team was the first to ever win a national championship for Seattle University. In both 1997 and 2004, Fewing received national coach of the year honors and produced national players of the year. In 2005, he received Fulcrum Foundation honors for being a champion of Catholic Education. For the past twenty-nine years, Peter has run the highly popular Peter Fewing Soccer Camp. From 2006-2008, he served as executive director of Seattle Scores teaching kids that they matter. Peter continues to serve on Seattle Scores board and on the advisory board of the Intercollegiate Athletic Leadership Program at the University of Washington. Besides being the head coach of the Kitsap Pumas, Fewing works as an announcer for the Seattle Sounders FC and ESPN radio.

Herbert (Herbie) Louis Hoffman III, Ph.D.

Hoffman has achieved distinction leading teams as military officer, an engineer and as a college soccer coach. In Desert Storm, Hoffman successfully led a team of ninety soldiers who had never worked together before. A West Point graduate, his military leadership awards include the Bronze Star and Ranger Tab. At Boeing, Hoffman continues to lead teams of up to twenty engineers from various disciplines. His team's efforts have resulted in numerous patents to include Boeing's Special Invention of the Year Award in 2005. Hoffman served as a men's assistant soccer coach at Seattle University from 1998-2006 where the team went undefeated and won a National Championship in 2004. In 2008, he earned his doctorate in leadership and policy studies from the University of Washington. As an instructor of the Team Leadership Certificate program at the University of Washington, Hoffman teaches a team development course for business leaders.

For information regarding speaking and/or coaching symposiums please go to: http://www.championshipteamsleadership.com/

Breinigsville, PA USA
21 December 2010
251971BV00002B/5/P